SPEAK WITH

THE EARTH AND

IT WILL TEACH YOU

~ ❀ ~

Speak with the Earth

and It Will Teach You

A Field Guide to the Bible

DANIEL COOPERRIDER

the pilgrim press

The Pilgrim Press
1300 East 9th Street
Cleveland, Ohio 44114
thepilgrimpress.com

Published 2022.

Scripture quotations, unless otherwise noted, are from the New Revised Standard Version of the Bible, © 1989 by the Division of Christian Education of the National Council of Churches of Christ in the United States of America. Used by permission. Changes have been made for inclusivity.

Printed on acid-free paper.

Library of Congress Cataloging-in-Publication Data on file.
LCCN: 2022939061

ISBN 978-0-8298-0014-2 (paper)
ISBN 978-0-8298-0015-9 (ebook)

Printed in The United States of America.

But ask the animals, and they will teach you,
　　the birds in the sky, and they will tell you;
or speak with the earth, and it will teach you,
　　and the fish of the sea will declare to you.
Who among all these does not know
　　that the hand of the Lord has done this?

—JOB 12: 7–9

I don't think it is enough appreciated how much an outdoor book the Bible is. It is a "hypaethral book," such as Thoreau talked about—a book open to the sky. It is best read and understood outdoors, and the farther outdoors the better. Or that has been my experience of it. Passages that within walls seem improbable or incredible, outdoors seem merely natural. This is because outdoors we are confronted everywhere with wonders; we see that the miraculous is not extraordinary but the common mode of existence. It is our daily bread.

—WENDELL BERRY

There is only one world, a world that God loves.
Since God loves it, we not only can but should. In fact, loving the world (not God alone), or rather, loving God through loving the world, is the Christian way.

—SALLIE MCFAGUE

The beauty of the world is Christ's tender smile
for us coming through matter.

—SIMONE WEIL

I am eager to report the glory of the universe;
may I be worthy to do it.

—HENRY DAVID THOREAU

CONTENTS

PART IV ❀ CLOUDS

ACKNOWLEDGMENTS

When I wrote the bulk of this book, I was living in Vermont, and I hope this writing bears the mark of that landscape with its blazing maples, dark green moss and fern-floored mountains, cold trout streams, big east-west skies, and fertile valleys. Any beauty in this book is inspired by the beauty that abounds in the Green Mountain State, including in the faith community of the Weybridge Congregational Church that prompted the idea of this book and journeyed with me through its initial stages. Towards the end of the project, my partner Julia and I moved to the Driftless hills of Wisconsin west of Madison with our soon-to-be-born daughter Reverie as Julia began as Senior Pastor of the Orchard Ridge UCC Church in Madison. Moving to Wisconsin has been a homecoming for me, as I grew up spending a few months a year at my family's cabin in the Wisconsin Northwoods, summer and winter. The imprint of the Wisconsin landscape, especially the ancient and enigmatic driftless area in the southwest, and the glaciated, boreal forests, bogs, lakes, and rivers up north, is also, I hope, apparent. In both landscapes, the earth element is on full and glorious display. Both landscapes have seduced me. Both landscapes compel me to speak up on their behalf, and on

ACKNOWLEDGMENTS

behalf of the earth itself, as we face our era of unprecedented ecological challenges and opportunities.

As I believe that in the end it is our love for the world that will inspire our most creative and compassionate dwelling on the earth, this is first and foremost a book of love. And so I dedicate it to the three great loves that inspired and sustained me during this project: love of creation and of the earth, love of the Weybridge Church (aka the Weybridge Wanderers), and love of Julia and Reverie, my sun and moon and stars.

PROLOGUE
God's Two Books

LEMON FAIR RIVER, VERMONT

Speak with the earth, and it will teach you . . .

—JOB 12:8

From the west-facing sunroom of my cabin-sized perch in Vermont's Champlain Valley, I look out on a muddy river slimmed to its summer banks, hills of mixed hardwood and clayplain forest crowned with distant Adirondack peaks, cumulus and a tower of cumulus congestus climbing into cobalt sky, and cloud shadows drifting across fields of clover and wild carrot. Although I've never seen a day quite like this one, the landscape immediately strikes a chord of intelligibility and integrity. With an emptying mind beginning to mirror the landscape, I feel myself belonging again, enfolded into a world that makes sense, a world that holds together with meaning: rivers making their way to the sea, clouds forming over ocean currents, rain falling on the mountains and running again as creeks and streams, forest communities clinging to the riverbanks and venturing inland. While we humans might wonder whether life has any meaning, the world itself coheres. "In my room," as poet Wallace Stevens wrote, "the world is beyond my understanding; / But when I walk I see that it consists of three or four / hills and a cloud."

A few miles downstream from here, near where the Lemon Fair River empties into Otter Creek, the Weybridge Congregational Church sits on its own hillside perch across the valley from Snake Mountain. It was almost a decade ago now that this small Open & Affirming, Creation Justice congregation of the United Church of Christ (UCC) welcomed me as their then twenty-seven-year-old pastor. Having studied theology and begun to get my feet wet in pastoral ministry in Chicago and Boston, moving to rural Vermont was a dramatic shift in context. For my first few years with the church, I operated largely as I had been educated to operate—that is, as an interpreter of the sacred text of the faith tradition within the traditions and context of the local community. Each week I turned to the Revised Common Lectionary and read the assigned scripture passages. I read commentaries on those passages, and commentaries on those commentaries. I held the Bible in one hand and the newspaper in the other. And then each Sunday I gathered together whatever I could glean from that reading to share with the community, offering the sermon like a word casserole at a homiletic potluck.

It took me a few years to realize that while I was focused on reading and interpreting layers of written text, the congregation was engaged in a different type of reading. On Sunday mornings, I would stand up and announce the lectionary calendar for the week—today is the First Sunday of Advent, today is the Eighth Sunday of Ordinary Time, today is Pentecost. After my words of welcome, we would open the microphone up to share joys and celebrations. Slowly I came to realize that during this time the congregation would announce and celebrate a different type of calendar, and speak to a different way of locating where we were in the spiritual journey of the year. "Today I celebrate my first bluebird sighting!" (Today is the First Sunday of True Spring). "This week I took a meandering drive through the mountains and the fall colors were magnificent!" (Today is the Sunday of Peak Leaves). "Today I celebrate hearing the grouse again in my woods." (Today is the First Sunday of the Grouse Drumming). "Today I celebrate the sound of wild geese calling overhead." (Today is the Third Sunday of either Stick Season or Mud Season, depending on whether the geese are leaving or returning, late fall or early spring). While I thought we were following the church lectionary and were reading from the calendar of assigned texts, this Vermont church, more attuned to the local earth than I was, taught me that our journey was also one of following the phenological calendar—the calendar of when things happen on the landscape—and that as a community we were reading together from this eco-liturgical lectionary for glimpses of God in the seasons of the natural world and its cycle of happenings.

Trained in philosophy, theology, and biblical hermeneutics, I was educated in that venerable, thousands-years-old tradition of humans searching for God and meaning by way of turning towards the written word and sorting out layer upon layer of textual meaning, sifting through written words about written words about written words. Every now and then one might find a word or an interpretation of a word worth its weight in gold, and so the intellectual, hermeneutical search can take on the feel of a treasure hunt. Slowly, slowly, my Vermont church taught me that there was a different way of reading for God and meaning. Slowly, slowly, they showed me what it looked like and felt like to read for God in the landscape and events of the earth. They taught me that the church was not just a place to read and interpret the written scriptures of God, but a place to read and interpret the expressions of God that emanate constantly and from every corner of God's creation.

※ ※ ※

PROLOGUE

Some people, in order to discover God, read books. But there is a great book: the very appearance of created things. Look above you! Look below you! Note it, Read it. God, whom you want to discover never wrote that book with ink. Instead, God set before your eyes the things that God had made. Can you ask for a louder voice than that? Why, heaven and earth shout to you: "God made me!"

—Augustine of Hippo

As human beings, we are given at least one, and often more than one window onto the world. We listen and the world sounds. We look and things appear and stand out in their thisness. We touch, smell, taste, and breathe in through our lungs and our skin and are in constant commerce and conversation with that which is beyond us. Ever since the earth started sensing itself and the universe through these human windows, the things that appeared and that spoke to our senses constellated themselves into the material of our stories and creative expressions. In other words, the things of the world are the means by which we know what we know and by which we move towards what we don't know. First things first, we are always and already in contact with the world—earthlings eating and exploring the things of earth—and only afterwards do we wonder about the world, becoming that part of the earth that turns its gaze back upon itself. Religion, philosophy, science, economics, and culture are all secondary and derivative productions of our earthiness, which is primal, primary, and generative.

Ancient Greek philosophers called this essential congruity between humanity and nature *logos*—similar to, but not exactly the same as, concepts such as order, reason, truth, *dharma*. Since the same logos that pervades nature pervades the human being as well, we, as part of a coherent universe, are capable of using our reason to understand and align ourselves with the ways of nature. Around the time of Jesus, this key philosophical term was gaining theological resonance as well, as in the writing of Hellenistic Jewish thinker Philo of Alexandria, for whom *logos* came to signify both the reason and order of the world as God made it to be as well as a type of intermediary figure or interpretive key that makes it possible to bridge the gap between creation and the Creator, and between humanity and God.

It's against this rich, centuries' long conversation on the meaning of *logos* that the author of the Gospel of John makes a decisive move to identify the Christ figure with *logos* in John 1:1, setting the stage for early Christian theologians to argue that the same *logos* incarnate as Christ is pervasive throughout nature and throughout scripture. Theologians like Justin Martyr (ca. 100–ca. 165), Irenaeus (ca. 130–ca. 202), and Origen (ca. 184–ca. 253) began developing the notion of Christ as *logos*, and each argued against certain spiritual impulses that viewed the material world as evil or cursed by affirming both the Hebrew Bible's notion of the original goodness and blessing of creation and the New Testament's vision of the incarnation—of God becoming flesh, of the divine fully embracing materiality by becoming it. Although they didn't use this phrase yet, the seeds of what is called the "two books" theory of God stretch back to the beginnings of Christian theology—the idea or metaphor that God writes or inspires not one book, but two: the book of nature and the book of scripture.

Beginning at least as early as Augustine of Hippo (354–430), the two books theory became more explicitly formulated and affirmed. For example, even before Augustine wrote about the "great book" that consists of "the very appearance of created things," the desert monk Anthony of Egypt (251–356) was preaching about the book of nature. When a philosopher visited him in the desert and asked him how such a learned person could live in the desert without the benefit of books, Anthony responded: "My book is the nature of created things, and as often as I have a mind to read the words of God, they are at my hand."

The two books tradition was developed into the medieval period by theologians like Maximus the Confessor, John Scotus Eriugena,

Hugh of Saint Victor, Hildegard von Bingen, Thomas Aquinas, Bonaventure, and Meister Eckhart. Rather than two books, Eriugena, for example, used the image of two shoes. "Christ wears 'two shoes' in the world: Scripture and nature," he wrote. "Both are necessary to understand the Lord, and at no stage can creation be seen as a separation of things from God." Meister Eckhart looked at a caterpillar and saw that "every single creature is full of God and is a book about God." "If I spent enough time with the tiniest creature—even a caterpillar," he wrote, "I would never have to prepare a sermon. So full of God is every creature."

Eckhart and other medieval mystics speak of a world that is thoroughly ecosemiotic, wherein every aspect of the world—from the insects on the ground to the stars in the sky—is saturated with theological meaning, each thing bearing the Creator's signature. Aquinas, steeped in the Aristotelian project of trying to understand the immediate, material world as it appears to our senses, also affirmed the study of the book of nature. Arguing against the spiritualist impulse to skip over the material world and focus solely on the otherworldly, Aquinas argued that knowledge of creation and of the creatures was essential to knowledge of God. With a simple declaration that reads haunting and prophetic for our age of climate chaos and anthropogenic ecological peril, Aquinas wrote that "a mistake about creation is a mistake about God."

During the Reformation, Luther and Calvin both embraced and also started to distance their theologies from the two books theory. While one can see Luther's embrace of the book of nature in his emphasis on the incarnation and in his own affirmation of the everyday sacrality of creaturely and bodily life, it is his understanding of what he called "The Real Presence of Christ" in the sacrament of communion that has the greatest implications for the two books theory. With his "Real Presence" theory, Luther was seeking a way to reconcile the simple, declarative statement from the communion ritual—when Jesus says, "This is my body"—with the post-Ascension scriptures that describe Jesus as being "at the right hand of God" (for example, Ephesians 1:20–23).

The theological dilemma and debate at the time was: if Christ is seated at the right hand of God, how then can Christ be present in the bread and wine as well? With his Real Presence theory, Luther was arguing on two fronts—first, against other reformers like Calvin, who claimed that Christ was only symbolically present in the elements, as well as against the Roman Catholic Church's position of transubstantiation, which argued that in the moment of consecrating the elements, the priest effects a sudden and complete change in the essential nature of the elements such that the bread is no longer bread but Christ's body, and the wine is no longer wine but Christ's blood. Luther—steeped in the Psalms and the image we find there of God's hand signifying God's steadfast presence everywhere, throughout the whole earth (see Psalm 139:7–10)—argued that *yes*, Christ is at God's right hand, and since God's right hand is everywhere and within everything, Christ also is present everywhere and in everything. And so for Luther, bread didn't have to be miraculously turned into Christ because bread already was Christ, and not in a figurative or symbolic way, but literally, physically, materially. In other words, the material world was thoroughly saturated with the presence of the sacred. To illustrate how bread could be both bread and Christ at the same time, he used the image of the iron on a blacksmith's anvil: the red-hot iron is simultaneously both iron and fire. "The power of God must be essentially present in all places, even the tiniest leaf," he wrote, "[which means] Christ is around us and in us in all places . . . Christ is present in all creatures, and I might find him in stone, in fire, in water, or even a rope."

With Calvin we also find a significant embrace of the two books theory. Following Paul in Romans 1:20, Calvin argued that all humans, through their encounter with the natural world, should be able to experience enough in that encounter with nature alone to know God. *Sensus divinitas*—a sense of the divine, as he called it—was an essential part of being human. Nature, as Calvin imagined it in his favorite metaphor, is like a theater where God's glory is constantly on display. And yet, on account of human sin we do not know God fully in nature, nor see God clearly on display as we should. The greatest sin, in Calvin's view, is not found among the seven deadly sins of pride, sloth, avarice, etc., but is instead the dulling of our sense perceptions that makes it difficult to sense God in nature. Therefore, Calvin argues, God gave us the second book, not only the "general revelation" of nature, as it was called, but the "special revelation" of the Bible.

Interestingly, although Luther based his argument on grace rather than sin, asserting that Christians did not need the intermediary of the priest to learn about God but could study God directly for themselves, he also came to the conclusion that it was the Bible alone that was needed for salvation, *sola scriptura*. With Luther's German Bible and Calvin's Geneva Bible, among other translations into the vernacular, the Reformation set the stage not only for the revolutionary forces of democracy, capitalism, and the industrial revolution, but also the unmistakable and unquestioned prioritization of the second book (the written book of scripture) over and above the first book (the living book of nature).

Over the course of the next few centuries in Western thought, generally speaking, the two books went their separate ways. Theologians tended to focus more and more on the book of scripture and less and less on the book of nature. Scientists like Galileo, Francis Bacon, and Charles Darwin embraced the metaphor of the book of nature, but they read it in a different way and for different purposes. The book of scripture was thought to lead to knowledge about spiritual reality, while the book of nature was thought to reveal material reality, as if the spiritual didn't arise from and express itself in the material, or as if the material weren't charged with the creativity and animating principle of *spiritus*. Once spirit and matter were split in this epistemological, intellectual sense, and once spirit was elevated above matter in the realm of religion, values, and ethics, it became possible to assault and abuse the material realm at a scale and pace that the world had never seen—or rather, that the earth had never witnessed. In relegating the interpretation of the sacred to the book of scripture, in looking for God only in words written by humans, Western thought embarked on a course of anthropocentric hermeneutics that has resulted in widespread disregard for nature's diverse otherness, leading to the climate chaos and mass species extinction that now characterizes the Anthropocene we have officially commenced.

✳ ✳ ✳

I wish to speak a word for Nature, for absolute freedom and wildness, as contrasted with a freedom and culture merely civil—to regard man as an inhabitant, or a part and parcel of Nature, rather than a member of society. I wish to make an extreme statement, if so I may make an emphatic one, for there are enough champions of civilization: the minister and the school committee and every one of you will take care of that.

—Henry David Thoreau, "Walking"

Not only do Christians and Christian theologians tend to seek God primarily in the book of scripture, but in the book of scripture itself we tend to focus only on the human characters. The classical phrase for this in theology is *Incurvatus in Se*, the self turned in on itself. We look for ourselves in all things, even in God. To try to understand God by way of reading and reflecting on words written by humans about humans would be like trying to understand a forest by walking around Manhattan and staring up at the human-built canopy of skyscrapers. In doing so, we might learn something about human nature, but not about forest nature.

Somewhere along the way, it seems, we've confused the order and the relationship between God's two books. We've denigrated the book of nature and exalted the book of scripture. We've thought that scripture was the key to understanding nature, and not vice versa. We've forgotten how the book of scripture—as beautiful as it can be—is but the slimmest of volumes that makes up the shortest of chapters in the epic, sprawling tome that is the book of nature. The world in all of its immediacy, diversity, and untamed extravagance could never be made to fit into a narrative plot nor a single volume bound by two covers. It is a book containing all things, even the uncontainability and unobtainability of the idea of God. When it comes to reading the book of nature, we haven't even begun to turn the first page.

What if we were to take the two books theory seriously again? Rather than try to reconcile the two books (there has been enough written about the relationship between "science" and "religion"), what if we were to swing the pendulum back and refocus on the book of nature as primary? Like Thoreau, what if we were to "speak a word for Nature," especially as it relates to our quest for understanding God and for navigating the territory of the spiritual life and its ethical summons during our era of climate crisis? That is the aim of this book: to "speak with the earth," as the book of Job puts it, to turn again towards creation in hopes of learning about the Creator, to return our attention to God's first book in order to listen and try to recover what we may be presently overlooking in our narrowed focus on the second book and its human concerns in an age where the earth is calling out with a clear but mute cry for us to think beyond ourselves and to seek the flourishing of the whole to which we are bound and to which we belong.

To that end I offer here a type of "field guide to the Bible." This is not a naturalist's field guide á la Audubon or Peterson, although I hope it shares something of their plein air invitation to get out there and explore, perhaps with book in hand, and see for yourself the wonders of the world. While there are resources that one can find along those lines, my aim is not to document and describe the flora and fauna recorded in the Bible. My aim is to reread the Bible in a living, breathing, yearning, determined search for God from the perspective of nature. My aim is not to read the book of nature through the lens of scripture, as has been a major trend in Christian theology, but the opposite—to read the book of scripture through the lens of the book of nature, to foreground the presence of the natural world, and to focus on creation and the more-than-human drama of life as it presents itself in its elemental forms.

To this end, the four major sections of this book reflect the four classical elements (water, fire, earth, air), and correspond to four prominent aspects of nature that hold powerful sway in the stories of scripture: Rivers, Mountains, Trees, and Clouds. These sections could well have been focused on other aspects of nature. The ones chosen here were simply the aspects of the world that spoke most clearly to me when I was envisioning and working on this project.

The essays that follow are essays in the literal, etymological, adventurous sense of the word—attempts at reading nature by being a body in nature, attempts at reading the first book as it makes its presence known and shapes the second book of scripture from within. While these are essays of constructive theology, they are not arguments in the academic sense. I aim to enact ecological hermeneutics and to give expression to a type of contemporary creation spirituality. My hope and prayer is that by reading differently, we can live differently.

The story we have been reading and telling about who we are and who God is and what the world is like has proven inadequate, small, and self-destructive. "A mistake about creation," as Aquinas put it, "is a mistake about God." And yet, I am hopeful and excited to share this work as a small part in this great conversation of our times because we are only beginning to understand and return proper attention to the book of nature. There is so much yet to discover, so many new pages to read. I trust that deep in the story and poetry of the book of nature there is more than enough life-giving and life-changing revelation to transform how curious creatures like us see the world and make meaning and beauty and action and care of it. I trust there is enough to change how we live in the world. I trust there is enough to lead us ever deeper in love and knowledge of the God in whom we live and move and have our being, if we but draw close to the glory of God in all of God's creations; if we but speak and listen and learn with the earth, as earth and in passionate, intimate conversation with earth—earth to earth.

RIVERS

CREATION ELEMENT INTERLUDE: WATER

. . . by the word of God heavens existed long ago
and an earth was formed out of water
and by means of water.

—2 PETER 3:5

In the beginning, when the earth was formless and void, and darkness covered the face of the deep, a wind from God swept over the surface of the waters. In the beginning, the earth was not yet, and as the surplus of the sudden flaring forth was settling, one of the massive clouds of dust and gas collapsed to form our solar system. At the center, the sun-ball formed into place like a gemstone, and as the dusty halo spun around it, a molten earth cooled into shape. Ice-filled and water-logged asteroids bombarded the young planet, and hydrogen from the solar cloud joined with oxygen in the atmosphere, and water, the liquid of life, arrived in abundance on earth. A billion years later, as the primordial soup of water and earth was simmering, life emerged and started to breathe. The atmosphere heaved with oxygen, as clouds and ocean vents and rain and rivers filled the planet up with water like a bathtub. Over the course of billions of water-bound years, single-celled organisms fused and became multicellular. Multicellular beings diversified and exploded into an array of swimming invertebrates. Around 530 million years ago, centipede-like animals started to explore the world beyond water. About 430 million years ago, the windswept plant spores started to take root on dry land, bringing their need for water with them as they ventured into the landlocked areas. About 400 million years ago, prehistoric fish creatures began crawling out of the seas, also bringing their need for water with them. We humans trace our lineage to these crawling fish, as life pulled itself up onto the earth from its watery, wave-tossed first phase in the seas.

As with the evolution of life in general, so each individual human life begins in the amniotic waters of the womb. And so, it is not surprising that whenever humans have wondered about where creation came from, we have tended to trace the story back to water in one way or another. "Water symbolizes the whole of potentiality," as Mircea Eliade writes in *Patterns in Comparative Religion*. "It is *fons et origo*, the source of all possible existence."

In the Bible, the creation myth of Genesis 1 is paradigmatic of cosmogonies we find around the world that trace the world's origins to water. Genesis imagines the water element to have been already present, there before God even begins. Before there was an earth, before there was light, the only thing that existed was water, and God's breath, which hovered over and started to stir the dark liquid like an artist starting to stir and mix their paint pallet. Water, then, is imagined as the original medium of creation, the source material. Water, in this sense, is the condition for beginning, for newness, for something to start happening.

We begin our life in water, and when we are born, we are born into a world of water. It covers about seventy-one percent of the earth's surface. The human body is similarly waterlogged, although the exact percentage changes throughout the course of our lives. We are about eighty percent water at birth. By the time our allotted span of days is over, we might find ourselves down to about fifty percent. Rather than an hourglass filled with falling sand, a bathtub emptying of water or a sponge being squeezed slowly dry might better speak to our mortality and the quickly diminishing or desiccating number of our days.

Given the abundance of water, it is one of the great climate tragedies of our time that water is quickly becoming one of the most important issues of environmental justice. Current estimates are that about one billion people don't have access to clean, fresh water sources, and that in the next decade roughly half the world's population will be facing a crisis in terms of water access. "In the desert," as the old Arabian proverb goes, "water is worth more than gold."

Both scarce and abundant, the water element can hold and transcend contradictions and dualities. Clean drinking water is essential to us humans and to all other animals and plants, and yet it provides nothing by way of energy or calories or organic nutrients. Water is odorless and tasteless in its pure form and yet it can quench and satisfy our deepest thirst. "The universal solvent," water can cleanse and dissolve and disintegrate almost every other substance—and yet it's also the most generative and nourishing substance. Water can destroy and create, break down and build up. The rain of a thousand years that carves out the Grand Canyon is the same rain that powers the growth of the 400-foot California Redwood, the "Thousand Year Pine."

"Nothing in the world is softer or weaker than water," as the *Tao Te Ching* puts it, "yet nothing is better at overcoming the hard and strong." And so water teaches the softness within us that what is soft is strong. Water teaches us how to yield and flow creatively when we encounter something difficult on our way. Through a path of non-resistance, water overcomes all obstacles.

Water is the least resistant to change of all the elements. It is the only element that can co-exist on earth in three different states at once—as a liquid, as a solid, and as vapor. It is this ease with which water is willing to change states that leads mythologically to the Greek god Proteus, the god of the sea, and the god from whom we get our word protean—ever-changing, mutable, fluid, adaptable, multifaceted.

As one of the main elemental ways that God visits the earth, water saturates the pages of the Bible in many forms—rain, lake, well, sea, drink. It's the river, though, that seems to hold a claim to primacy. This isn't much of a surprise—a river is water in its most alive, most animated, most protean form. "Let the rivers clap their hands," Psalm 98 proclaims, and indeed a river is water moving and dancing across the landscape, bringing life and joy wherever it goes. When it meets rocks or ledges, the river claps and sings and like the blues turns the experience of obstacle into haunting beauty. "Who hears the rippling of rivers," as Thoreau put it, "will not utterly despair of anything."

In the spiritual landscape of the Bible—to borrow the phrase from Norman Maclean's classic story of fly fishing in Montana—a river runs through it. It's there in the beginning, right in the middle of the garden of Eden, and a river is there at the end, right in the middle of the heavenly city, the New Jerusalem. God visits the earth as water again and again, and often in the shape of a river, a stream of mercy, a flow of grace, a river of the water of life.

I

THE SOURCE
RIVERS OF PARADISE

When you go deep, following a winding river to its source,
you're soon bewildered, wandering a place beyond knowing:
cragged peaks towering above stay lost in confusions of mist,
and depths sunken away far below surge and swell in a blur.

—HSIEH LING-YUN (385–433),
TRANSLATED BY DAVID HINTON

Who are we? Where are we? Why are we? When we open the Bible to the first chapter of Genesis, we're brought immediately into the wonder of those first order questions of existence. "This is the account," as the opening words put it, "of the heavens and the earth when they were created." Of course, not even the best of our modern scientific knowledge can get us back to that very first moment of creation, let alone tell us why, or from where such a beginning could come, and so we turn to poetry, metaphor, imagination, history, and art to try to get close to the beginning, to try to get close to the source and origin of life, to the beginning that was with God.

When the ancient poets of Genesis 1–2 turned their creative focus to the question of origin and source, they found their imaginations led back to the image of water, and of God's spirit on the dawn of creation "hovering over the waters" (Genesis 1:1), beginning to stir the world into being from its formless, watery start. Nearly half the verses in the opening hymn to creation have something to do with water, and particularly with flowing water, with streams and rivers, with "living water," as it's called, reflecting how rivers can have the feeling of a living being moving through the landscape.

Living water continues to connect us to thoughts of origin and source. "Is there water there?" is often the first question we ask about a new planet that might support life, reflecting the basic, essential connection between water and life, and particularly the type of clean and running water that rivers represent. And so, we find that in places and cultures ranging from the Yellow River in China to the Mekong in Southeast Asia to the Danube in Europe, rivers are often referred to in the local languages as Mother. Rivers—living, flowing water—speak to us intimations of mother, source, beginning. I think about the beautiful last paragraph of *On the Origin of Species*, in which Darwin sits by a riverside and ponders what he calls "the tangled bank" of life, awed by the diversity of forms that spring up on the banks of a river, the plants, the insects above and underground, the birds flitting in the bushes. "From so simple a beginning," he wrote by that English riverside, "endless forms most beautiful and most wonderful have been, and are being evolved."

When we think back on it, many of the milestones of human history have taken place along the banks of rivers. The 200,000-year-old fossilized remains of our earliest known hominid ancestors were found along the banks of Ethiopia's Awash River. Ten thousand years ago, the momentous paradigm shift from a hunter-gatherer to an agricultural way of life happened in the Fertile Crescent Valley between the Tigris and Euphrates Rivers in Mesopotamia, the "cradle of civilization." And then, after having explored and settled much of the world by way of river navigation, a couple hundred years ago the rivers of England, and then later of America, ushered in a new technological age with the river mills that powered the Industrial Revolution. Today, the Mississippi River generates over 400 billion dollars annually in river commerce and supports 1.3 million jobs. Over two thirds of the world's drinking water comes from rivers and streams. Hydropower is the most widely used renewable energy source. While human population density has long congregated along rivers, recent demographic analysis suggests that perhaps we are beginning to move a bit further from the riverbank, as climate induced flood events threaten civilization in ways perhaps never before seen.

※ ※ ※

As Genesis 2 opens, there is a sense of a preexistent barrenness or aridness to the world. When God started creating things this time around, at first there was a sense of only that which was lacking—"no plant of the field was yet in the earth and no herb of the field had yet sprung up" (Genesis 2:5). But then suddenly, in the next verse, "streams came up from the earth and watered the whole surface of the ground," and that's when things start to take off (Genesis 2:6). The picture that Genesis 2 paints is that in Eden, at the very beginning, we lived in an idyllic garden setting. Everything was beautiful and abundant and pure and good. When the text continues on to describe the features of the Garden of Eden, at the heart of the garden as if it is the crowning achievement of creation and so given more verses than any other aspect of Eden, we find the first river of life:

> A river flows out of Eden to water the garden, and from there
> it divides and becomes four branches.
>
> —Genesis 2:10

This paragraph of scripture has long enchanted and perplexed readers. While most of the descriptions of Eden feel mythical and unreal, when the text describes the rivers that flow from Eden—known poetically as the "rivers of paradise"—the story seems to take a geographical, historical, and literal turn that is both intriguing and baffling.

The river of life splits into four branches. The four rivers are given names and descriptions, and while two of them are clearly real rivers known to the area, the Tigris and the Euphrates, the other two are mysterious and unknown Hebrew names, the Pishon and the Gihon. Of course, the mystery of these two rivers has only added to the intrigue, as deciphering the location of these rivers would hold the key to discovering where the Garden of Eden was located. The Nile, the Ganges, the Mississippi, the North Pole, even the Milky Way, with its four arms and its Chinese name as the Silver River of Heaven— all these and more have been theories proposed for where and what these four rivers of Eden, these four rivers of paradise, could have been referring to. In the Quran, the prophet Muhammad was also given the vision of the four rivers of paradise. Two of the rivers were real and visible, in this case the Nile and the Euphrates, while the other two were said to be intentionally hidden and invisible—spiritual, rather than literal, rivers of paradise. We find a similar riparian mythology in northern India, where another holy place, the Triveni Sangam, lies at the confluence of three sacred rivers and is said to be the place where one can wash away one's sins and find freedom from the cycle of death and rebirth. Here the Ganges, Yamuna, and Sarasvati rivers merge, the first two being visible and real on the earth, the third being invisible and mythical. At the heart of holiness, it seems, at the source of the sacred, we find the joining of the visible with the invisible, the confluence of the manifest with the unmanifest, the real with the more-than-real.

* * *

Rivers, by their very nature of having to begin somewhere, reflect to us the mystery of source. Stiller bodies of water, like lakes and oceans, can seem self-contained and self-sufficient compared to a river. When I stand at the edge of the ocean, my wonder is more about the beyond of the horizon than about the beginning. I can look out on a pond and trace the entire outline of it. A river, on the other hand, is more difficult to comprehend in one glance. When I picture a river, I tend to picture it in its middle course, a channel of moving water twisting, turning, and meandering through the landscape, sometimes quickly with rapids, sometimes slowly with deep pools. But a river is also an estuary where it empties into an ocean or a lake. And a river, whether it begins as a spring or as snowmelt or as rain runoff, is also its source.

I found myself called to pastor my first church in Weybridge, Vermont, a small town in the Champlain Valley founded because of its auspicious location along Otter Creek, situated near three of its powerful waterfalls. One day in midsummer's mosquito and black fly season, I set out to try to find the source of Otter Creek. At over 100 miles long, it is Vermont's longest river. Bordered to the east by the Green Mountains and to the west by the Taconic Mountains, Otter Creek has long been a major highway for humans and other wildlife connecting Lake Champlain to southern New England. The Abenaki named this river Onegilwizbo, meaning Otter River, and also Bikogtegw, meaning Crooked River, which fits with the river's often lackadaisical meandering through the landscape, full of sweeping oxbows.

The question of the source of Otter Creek is unsettled. Guidebooks often trace Otter Creek back to Emerald Lake in Dorset, Vermont. In my search for its source, I stopped first at the small outflowing stream on the north side of the lake, and it did look like a miniature version of the river that I knew further downstream—a self-contained river winding its way confidently and unhurriedly between clearly defined banks over and around rocks and trees. I looked at a more detailed topographical map of the area, though, and I saw that there's a stream flowing into Emerald Lake that on some GPS systems is also called Otter Creek. I visited that little creek right before it enters the lake, and while smaller and more tangled with alders and willows, it still looked, again, mostly like a miniature version of the Otter Creek that I knew.

I looked at my map again and traced the little blue line upstream. Just a couple of miles south of Emerald Lake, the stream takes a sharp turn east and north as the tributary climbs up Mount Tabor. Named after a prominent monadnock in Galilee where the Transfiguration of Christ was said to occur, Mount Tabor in Vermont seems to lack such prominence and fades into the background, one of many lush green mountains that rise and fall north-south along the spine of the state.

With a bottle of water, a notebook, and an apple or two foraged from the nearby Mad Tom Orchard, I set off on foot to find the source. Other duties kept me from getting to this spot until late in the afternoon, so I was a bit up against time and light. I set an alarm for an hour, figuring that, with a little extra time for meandering, I had a little less than three hours of light left in the day.

Unlike its deep and muddy phase near where I live, at the base of Mt. Tabor Otter Creek is cold and clear. It looks like the mountain streams that I love to fish for native brook trout. And so, for the first stretch, I was reading the river as if I were fishing. Are there trout here? Is that bend deep enough? How would I position myself to make a cast for this run? Do I see any bugs coming off the water?

The stream, alas, was too small to support trout. I turned my attention to the bank and found my first patch of golden chanterelles! But then I thought about the setting sun, and given the vigor of the stream, I worried the source might be miles away. I put my head down and proceeded to bound, as quickly as I could, up the hill, up the riverbed. The only things slowing me down were the gnats swarming my head, the stinging nettles burning my knees, the frogs spooking and jumping from nearly every pool, the bruised shin from slipping and crashing into some river rocks, the ferns and popple that wrapped around my bruised shin, the eerie feeling that I might run into a bear at any moment, or step on a porcupine.

I decided to get as high up the mountain and as close to the source as I could before my hour alarm went off. For the first stretch, it seemed hopeless, as the rocky riverbed seemed to go on and on without end. The first sign of hope that maybe I could actually make it to the source was when the sound of the stream changed, from the steady, full, white-noise rush of the falling lower mountain stream, to the gentle trickle of the upper mountain stream, a beautiful soft sound that felt bright in my body like the late afternoon light streaming and dappling on the river rocks and tangled bank.

As I got higher, and as the water got smaller, I noticed that there were stretches of the stream in which the river seemed to disappear, where the water went underground, or under rock for a bit, only to reemerge in another small pool and as another small cascading stream. Interesting, I thought, as I pushed on under the darkening forest canopy. Five minutes left. Still plenty of water. Still a frog jumping in each pool. Head down, I thought, as close to the source as I can get.

A little delirious at this point from the stinging nettles, the gnats, the bug spray, the immense, imponderable mystery of the Source and the question of Life and God in my head, I went up. I lost my footing at points, slipping and twisting, but somehow I did not break any bones or get trapped and die alone on Mount Tabor. And then my alarm sounded. Time to stop. Drenched in sweat, I sat down for my first drink of water. And when I sat down, I noticed that it was quiet. Deathly quiet, as they say. Quiet as in no insects, no frogs, no birds. Quiet as in no water.

I had somehow hiked past the source without knowing it. Or had I? The riverbed seemed to continue indefinitely up the mountain. And on my left and right, rocky tributaries seemed to be coming in, except without any visible water in them.

After catching my breath and rehydrating, I started slowly and gingerly back down the mountain, on hyper alert for where exactly this river system actually started. I saw some dampness in a mossy patch just below me, which looked more like a fairy home than a spring, but there was no standing or flowing water. Discovering where the water began with my eyes proved more difficult than listening to where the water began, as the drip drip, drop drop I heard a bit downstream turned out to be the closest thing I could find to a source. After minutes of careful attention, I can't say that I could discern exactly where the water came from. I don't know if it was a spring or the moisture from snow and rain. Water seemed to seep out of the rock itself, as if squeezed from a wet rag. It would then collect on one slim linchpin, a shard of rock wedged between the boulders from which water was dripping in well-defined droplets like from a leaky faucet. The sound pattern was steady and sure, like a metronome with a four-count rhythm.

I sat there for a while, close to what may or may not have been the source of Otter Creek. I listened and listened—drip drip, drop drop—wondering—could this be it? The confluence of the visible and the invisible that marks the heart of holiness? The source of the sacred that we both see and don't see, that we both hear and don't hear, or maybe better to say that the closer we get to seeing and hearing the further we are from knowing and sensing from whence and from where.

✳ ✳ ✳

The number four is a classic symbol of wholeness. Four represents everything. The four corners of the earth. The four directions of heaven. In a spiritual sense, the four rivers that flow out from Eden, visible and invisible, flow everywhere. All of life, in this sense, can be said to receive its life from paradise. This isn't to say that everything is perfect, of course, but like a drop of water becoming part of the river, everything has God's original perfection streaming through it.

Now, whenever I cross a river driving, or walking, or hiking, or paddling, or swimming, or whenever I open the faucet to take a drink from the flowing, living water, I hear the drip drip, drop drop from my search for the source of Otter Creek, and I am reminded that every river comes from the source of God, that every river is a river of paradise, and that in this clear cold original goodness everything visible and invisible mingles and merges into one.

2

MOTHER RIVER

If the earth is a mother then rivers are her veins.

—Amit Kalantri

etween two great unknowns we live our lives. Bubbling up as
from a hidden spring in the forest, our journey begins with
birth and the dark enigma of "from where?" As our lives grow,
we gain strength and momentum, we are fed by tributaries, we take
on a certain character and personality, we twist and turn and tumble
over ledges and sing as we go. And then at the end, we cease being
ourselves as we empty into the ocean of the all. River is our most natural, ready-to-hand metaphor for the journey of life because like our
lives, river names that part of the flow of water that is between the
beginning and the end. Derived from the Latin *riparia*, meaning the
bank or the shore on either side of the river, river is at heart a liminal
phenomenon, an in-between thing. The river separates the two banks,

making room for the water to flow between them, and it joins the two banks together again, making them integral to the landscape, carrying nutrients to the earth as arteries carry blood and energy in our bodies.

Given the deep connection between rivers and life, it is not surprising that when we look at the cultures and languages that have been born along the banks of the world's mighty rivers, in many of them we find traditions and myths referring to river as mother—the Yellow River in China, known as "Mother River"; the Volga River in Russia, known as "The Mother of the Land"; the Rio Madre de Dios, the River of the Mother of God in the Andes. The Thai word for river in general, *mae nan*, translates as "water mother." The Danube, the second largest river in Europe, has long been linked to the sacred feminine. Known as "Mother Danube," she is associated with the Celtic Goddess Danu, the maker of creation itself and source of the river from which all life comes.

※ ※ ※

The story of Moses's life as told in the book of Exodus begins along the tangled banks of the Nile. Either the longest or second longest river in the world, the Nile begins its journey either in the mountains of Burundi or Rwanda, depending on which source is acknowledged as the headwaters, and flows for more than 4,000 miles before emptying into the Mediterranean Sea. Today along its banks, eleven nations and over 300 million people find life. Along its banks, the ancient Egyptian civilization flourished for thousands of years. They didn't call this river the Nile, as that is its foreign, Greek name. They would address the river instead with reverence as in prayer, evoking her as a goddess with the title "The Mother of all Humanity."

A generation or two before Moses, because of an extended draught and famine in their homeland of Canaan, the Hebrew peoples, led by the patriarch Jacob and his son Joseph, migrated to Egypt in search of the greener pastures that the Nile River Valley provided as it flooded on a regular basis, bringing the rich dark earth from the Ethiopian mountains down into the arid plains of Egypt. The Egyptians referred to the regular and life-giving flooding of the Nile as "the tears of Isis," named after the mother goddess of healing and magic.

From the history as it's presented in the Biblical account, the relationship between the immigrant Hebrews and the native Egyptians seems to have been peaceful and mutually beneficial for a few generations. But then "a new king," (Exodus 1:8) who had no knowledge of Jacob and Joseph, came to power. And so, Exodus begins on an ominous tone. Next follows a formula that is all too familiar when it comes to totalitarian regimes. Wishing to secure his nativist base of support, the new ruler identifies a common enemy, a scapegoat on which to focus society's fear and insecurity. In this case, it's the Hebrew immigrants farming the land. The new king fears that the immigrants are becoming too powerful, and in response, first, he orders their workload increased, and second, he orders their male children slaughtered, drowned in the Nile.

Against the background of this attempted genocide, an undercurrent of resistance starts to take shape. Strikingly, it is the women who lead this undercurrent of resistance and civil disobedience, beginning with the Hebrew midwives and mothers who find ingenious ways to resist and defy the decrees of the Pharaoh, and then ending with the Pharaoh's own daughter who secretly adopts the Hebrew child, Moses. There's a rich irony here. While it's the men and male babies that the Pharaoh seems to fear the most, it's the women and mothers who are actually the powerful, revolutionary players here.

The moment when the Hebrew midwives and mothers work together to defy the Pharaoh (Exodus 1:15–21) is a significant moment and perhaps a turning point in the Bible. Up until this point, throughout the book of Genesis, the narrative of the Bible is decidedly patriarchal, dominated by the archetypal dreams and failings of a type of masculine power motivated by fear and pride and jealousy. The beginning of

Exodus is the first time when matriarchal power rises up in resistance and gifts us with an alternative way of being, the Hebrew women confounding the Pharaoh's fear and power with creativity and compassion. "We aren't able to kill the babies like you've asked, dear Pharaoh," they say with a wink. "Hebrew women are not like Egyptian women; they are vigorous and give birth before the midwives arrive" (Exodus 1:9). Here we witness the power in the sacred vocation of the mother and the midwife and the doula to bring forth and preserve new life in the world. Their vocationally inspired attempts to defy the Pharaoh's decree of death and save the Hebrew babies is nothing less than the first act of nonviolent civil disobedience for the sake of justice in the Bible. It is the beginning of a tradition that Martin Luther King, Jr. would later evoke when he cried out, in the words of the prophet Amos, "let justice roll down like a river, and righteousness like an ever-flowing stream" (Amos 5:24).

Into this current of women-led political resistance baby Moses is born. Exodus 2 describes how, right after Moses was born, his mother (not named here, but later identified as Jochebed) looked at him, and she saw that he was a "fine child" (Exodus 2:2). The translation is a bit misleading. The Hebrew reads more like, "she looked at the child and saw that it was good." This is the same phrasing that we find at the very beginning of Genesis, when after each day of creation, God looks out over everything that God has made, and God sees that it is good. It's a beautiful little detail in the Bible, that when Moses's mother looks at the newborn child, just as whenever we look upon new life, especially the face of a newborn child, that same original goodness and blessing of creation—"Eden's first light"—still shines through.

Given the original goodness and blessing of the child, Jochebed does her best to keep the child alive. First, she keeps the baby hidden for the first three months. But then there comes a point when she can no longer hide him. Babies, naturally, tend not to take vows of silence. Acting creatively and courageously, Jochebed makes a basket for her baby, weaving it out of papyrus growing along the riverside and sealing it with resin and pitch from other streamside plants and trees, and she hides Moses among the reeds along the banks of the Nile. Another interesting textual detail is hidden here. The same word that's translated as "basket" is translated earlier in Genesis as "ark," as in the ark that Noah built to survive the Great Flood. Just as Noah built an ark to save creation and humanity during the flood, so Moses's mother builds a mini-ark to save the one who would eventually be the leader and liberator of his people. The mother of Moses releases and trusts her child to the care of the "Mother of all Humanity." She puts her faith in the life-giving, life-flowing, life-saving waters of creation, trusting life will find a way to preserve life.

Jochebed's trust that good things would come from the river pays off in spectacular fashion. Just downstream from where she left the baby, the Pharaoh's daughter (unnamed here but later known in tradition as Bithia), comes down to the riverside to bathe. She sees the basket among the reeds, and moved by compassion, she knows in her heart that she cannot let the baby die. On a brilliant and daring stealth mission, Moses's older sister Miriam approaches the Pharaoh's daughter and informs her that she just happens to know of someone who could nurse the baby. In a narrative dripping with the most wonderful irony, the Pharaoh's daughter retrieves the Moses basket from the river and invites none other than Moses's real mother Jochebed to be the wet nurse for her newborn adopted child. She even offers to pay her, adding a final flourish to the dazzling matriarchal power on display in this story. Bithia names the infant boy Moses, which means "I drew him from the water" or "He came from the river."

And so it was that Moses the great prophet was born from many mothers, including from the wide, dark, rich, life-giving tears of Isis, the River Nile, the Mother of all Humanity.

3

LIVING WATERS
(DOWN IN THE RIVER TO PRAY)

By-and-by we'll all go down, all go down, all go down,
By-and-by we'll all go down,
Down in the river to pray.

—African-American Spiritual

As a pastor, performing a baptism is the most beautiful of ritual moments that I get to experience, although my favorite moment in the liturgy I am familiar with is lay led. As the presiding deacon at the Vermont church I served poured the water from the clear pitcher into the clear bowl, from a height in which the water splashed and gurgled as it fell down as if from a waterfall, they would say, alluding to Paul's interpretation of baptism being at once a death and a rebirth (Romans 6:4): "This is the water of baptism. Out of this water we rise with new life, forgiven of sin and one in Christ."

We think Jesus was baptized at thirty or thirty-one years old. We don't know much about him at this point in life other than that he was compelled to make a pilgrimage to visit John the Baptist out in the desert, who was preaching a bold and urgent message of dying to the old and lightless ways of the world and being reborn according to the radiant ways of God. Jesus made the trek south from Nazareth in the Sea of Galilee region, heading downstream along the Jordan River until he made it to the spot where the prophet John was baptizing people in the lower course of that river. Al-Maghtas is the Arabic name that's used today for the likely spot, meaning "immersion," and by extension, "baptism."

There, along what was likely then a wild and scenic stretch of the river a few miles upstream from where it empties into the Dead Sea, John was preaching a message of radical life-change, one that he marked by having people submerge and reemerge from the waters. With religious roots in the Jewish mikvah practice of taking a ritual bath to purify oneself, the type of baptism that John was practicing was understood in quite dramatic and existential terms to be a death and rebirth ritual. It was conceived of as a death of the old self and the old ways, as one held one's breath underwater in an experience of drawing close to death, and then came back up and out from the waters, reborn from the waters, gasping for breath, looking out at the world wild eyed and curious as if for the first time, renewed, reborn, sometimes renamed.

While mikvah baths are usually self-contained indoor structures, the one key ingredient for a traditional mikvah is that they contain at least a portion of "living water" (Hebrew: *mayyim chaim*), meaning flowing water as from a spring or river. "Living water" is a key term in the Hebrew Bible, including as a title for God in Jeremiah 2:13. Jesus, in his early encounter with the Samaritan woman at the well, hinted at the promise that living water had to quench all thirst and lead to eternal life, before later declaring himself to be that living water. "If anyone is thirsty," he said, "let them come to me and drink... Whoever believes in me... from their innermost being will flow rivers of living water" (John 7:37–39).

One aspect of what seems to have drawn people like Jesus to John was that John was re-wilding the traditional Jewish mikvah practice. By inviting people to gather by the riverside, and by inviting them to wade out and join him in the middle of the river, where the water was deepest and the current strongest, I imagine that Jesus—as a young person full of yearning and passion and hunger and thirst for truth and beauty and justice—first heard John's invitation to baptism in the Jordan as something like a call or summons to the wild and scenic river of life within him, saying: Do you want to encounter and be blessed by real living waters? Do you want to encounter the Creator through total immersion in Creation? Do you want to die to all the small ways and be reborn to ever-more expansive realities? Do you want to be blessed by the source or spring of Living Water itself—the eternal life-force that streams within all living things? Do you want to be baptized into the wildness and sacredness and beauty and goodness of this world? If so, join me down by the riverside—come down with me, down in the river to pray.

Jesus, along with many others, journeyed down to the riverside seeking out the wild-eyed river prophet who wore camel's hair and ate locusts and wild honey. There, Jesus had John dunk his body down under those living waters of the river, and when he came back up, it was indeed as if he was reborn. Immediately after emerging from the river, Jesus experienced the heavens opening and God's Spirit like a dove descending upon him, and the newly baptized was renamed and reclaimed as God's very own.

Martin Luther once remarked that he thought about his baptism every morning when he washed his face. He said that there was no greater assurance in this life than the assurance of baptism. The God who cannot lie said "Yes" to him, said, "You are my child. I will call you Beloved." In the prayer that Luther wrote for the baptismal liturgy, known as the "Flood Prayer," Luther compared the living waters of baptism to the flood waters from the time of Noah, writing that rather than being a flood of wrath, baptism represents a flood of mercy, a flood of grace. "Through the Baptism in the Jordan of Your beloved Son," he wrote, "You sanctified and instituted all waters to be a blessed flood, and a lavish washing away of sin." I'm struck by what's implied in the "all waters" idea. That baptism means that all water is holy water, that God's grace is mingled with and streams through every river, creek, brook, spring. Luther also wrote that in the event of baptism, "every Christian has enough to study and to practice for an entire lifetime."

Imagining Jesus in the Jordan, I wonder how that water-logged moment of being fully submerged in the river saturated the rest of his life. I wonder how often he thought about that moment, what wisdom he took from the living waters that pearled off his eyebrows and dripped from his chin as he reemerged, reborn.

✳ ✳ ✳

The Jordan River begins its journey deep in the mountains that form the border between Syria and Lebanon. It starts as a small mountain stream at an elevation of 9,232 feet. The upper course flows south and drops rapidly over its first sixty miles, tumbling and crashing down the mountainside before entering the Sea of Galilee (also known as the Kinneret), which lies at about 685 feet below sea level. The river exits the south side of the Sea of Galilee and continues south for eighty miles over a much less steep gradient, dropping only another 700 feet until it empties into the Dead Sea, near where Jesus was baptized, which is the lowest land on earth at nearly 1,400 feet below sea level.

Given the steep downward gradient, especially of its upper course, and given its inexorable push towards the lowest land surface on earth, it makes sense that the word Jordan, in its Hebrew etymology, means "to go down," or "to flow down," as of course, all rivers do. "The water seeks its own level," as the saying goes, as the laws of physics make the living waters of a river irresistibly self-propelled on their journey downstream, which means their journey of descent.

We find the same imagery of descent with the story of Jesus's baptism. First, he had to journey downstream from Galilee to find John. He found John near the mouth of the Jordan where the river emptied into the Dead Sea, down near the very lowest spot on this whole planet. Jesus had to go down the riverbank to John. He had to go down the bank and into the river. Once in the river, John plunged him down under the flowing water, totally immersing him under it. And then when Jesus came up for breath, the heavens opened and God's spirit came down, God's spirit descending upon him.

To go down, to flow down. It makes me wonder about the direction of God's activity and God's energy in the world. There is a significant strand of religion and spirituality that is what we could call a theology of ascent. The idea that the direction of God is up and beyond. The idea that we climb a ladder to get to God. That we get to God by striving, achieving. By pulling ourselves up, by upward mobility. That we get to God by lifting our thoughts above this earth, and eventually by having our souls ascend up to heaven after we die.

But when I hold this theology up to Jesus, I wonder if a theology of descent more accurately describes what he was up to, and what God's Spirit was up to, working in and with and through him. I think about how Jesus was always moving and teaching not up towards the mighty and the powerful, but down towards the last and the least. "Blessed are the poor in spirit." "Blessed are the meek or humble." I think about how our English word humble comes from the Latin *humilis*, "low, lowly," from *humus*, "ground."

There is a sense of the art of humility embedded in the accounts of his baptism as well. Matthew tells about John deferring to Jesus, saying, "I need to be baptized by you, and do you come to me?" (Matthew 3:14).

Luke writes about Jesus's posture of solidarity with the yearning masses when he writes that, "When all the people were being baptized, Jesus was baptized too" (Luke 3:21).

I think about the Jordan River's influence when I think about Jesus's love for the littlest and least, the mustard seed, the little children, the widow's mite. I think about Jesus bending down to wash his disciples' feet. I think about Mary Magdalene bending down to wipe Jesus's feet with her perfumed hair and tears. I think about the incarnation that is celebrated at Christmas, which is the other story of Jesus's birth in the Gospels, and which is a masterpiece narrative about how the love of God descends here to this earth, seeking out the lowest and the least as the place of God's birth into this world. And finally, I think about how, after his death, Jesus was placed underground in the tomb for three days. I think about how the Apostle's Creed describes this as Jesus "descending into hell," descending into the depths of the earth and the underworld.

❋ ❋ ❋

The Jordan River Valley is a landscape of inestimable ecological, cultural, and religious importance. Connecting the ecosystems of Asia and Africa, the river is a holy site for the more than 500 million migratory birds that follow its flow upstream and downstream each year. And it is a holy site for the billions of people who are part of the Jewish, Christian, and Muslim faith traditions who cherish the sacred stories that are set along its banks. It is also a special heritage for humanity as a whole, as its valley was one of the first places humans settled after migrating out of Africa, with the city Jericho being one of the earliest examples of our species' proclivity to agricultural-urban development. Along the river-greened banks of the Jordan, Jericho has a claim to being the oldest continually inhabited city on the planet.

And yet, in one of the most damning judgments about the state of our species' stewardship of the gifts of creation, today the Jordan River, particularly the lower stretch in which Jesus was baptized, is nearing ecological collapse. Over the past fifty years, ninety-six percent of the river's flow has been diverted. The seasonal trickle of water that remains is polluted with saline and effluent. It is estimated that a full half of the biodiversity has been lost. Family farms have seen their once fertile fields crumble into dust. The Dead Sea is drying up at the rate of about a meter a year. It is all so tragic that we can hardly face the truth of it, as it haunts us with an apocalyptic ecological wondering: if we as a species cannot take care of such an obviously sacred landscape, what part of the earth, if any, will we be able to keep beautiful and verdant for future generations?

✳ ✳ ✳

The way the living waters of a river flow down teaches us something, expresses something, preaches something about how God's energy, God's love, God's mercy flows down and floods every tiny little crack and corner of creation. "The supreme good," according to the *Tao Te Ching*, "is like water, which nourishes all things without making any effort. Water is content with the low places that people disdain. Thus it is like the Tao, or the Way, or the Truth."

Or as Jesus taught, drawing as I imagine now on the wisdom gained from his baptism in those downward flowing waters of the Jordan River, "those who exalt themselves shall be humbled, and those who humble themselves shall be exalted" (Luke 14:11). Jesus experienced and was inspired by the alchemical truth of rivers that we need in our age of climate change now more than ever—that rivers are places and means whereby old ways die and flow down and new ways can emerge and be born.

RIVERS

I think this hopeful thought while sitting down to pray next to a still wild and scenic river as the living waters sidestep and dance over and around rocks and ledges, as the water makes the most mesmerizing patterns of riffles, rapids, and eddies as it overcomes obstacles, as it seeps into all the cracks and crevices making its way down, down, down...

It is enough to study and practice for a lifetime.

4

APOCALYPTIC HOPE
WATERSHIP DISCIPLESHIP & THE ROUND RIVER

I would say that there exist a thousand unbreakable links between each of us and everything else, and that our dignity and our chances are one. The farthest star and the mud at our feet are a family; and there is no decency or sense in honoring one thing, or a few things, and then closing the list. The pine tree, the leopard, the Platte River, and ourselves—we are at risk together, or we are on our way to a sustainable world together. We are each other's destiny.

—Mary Oliver, Upstream: Selected Essays

Stories about rivers go back to the beginning of stories about anything, and the steady flow of time has worn the stories solid and smooth like the stones that line a riverbed. According to ancient Greek cosmogony, the River Okeanos flowed in a circle around the flat disk of the earth. It was the source of all the world's fresh water—all rivers, wells, springs, streams, lakes, clouds. Its source was a spring in a cave in which the immortals lived. The heavenly bodies—the sun and moon and stars—all rose from its waters and then returned to rest in them when their daily course was done. In the darkness, the sun god would sail around the river in a golden boat, beginning in the north, heading west, and continuing to float on the circular river before rising again in the east. Poets from Homer to Aeschylus sung praises to this round river whose stream circled back on itself. "Old Okeanos," as an Orphic hymn put it, "whose liquid arms begird the solid land."

I grew up canoeing the rivers in the Northwoods of Wisconsin. The Namekagon River was our backyard river only a few miles away. As the largest tributary of the St. Croix River, the Namekagon is part of the nationally protected St. Croix National Scenic Riverway. The other river where we would most often canoe and camp is the Bois Brule, which shares the same headwaters with the St. Croix in a dense boreal bog just north of Upper St. Croix Lake and Solon Springs, Wisconsin. There, a 2.3-mile-long section of the North Country Scenic Trail follows the historic portage between the two river systems. The Brule flows north, plunges over a series of ledges and falls, and empties into Lake Superior. The St. Croix flows southwest and empties into the Mississippi. This portage trail, used for generations by the Ojibwe, turned the Brule and the St. Croix River system into one of the most important highways on the continent. From here, one could head north to Gichigamiing, the great inland sea, and from there east to the St. Lawrence and the Atlantic Ocean beyond. Or one could head southwest towards the Mississippi and on down to the Gulf of Mexico. It made possible a circular journey in which one could start paddling in one direction and, without reversing course, eventually end up back where one started.

According to Wisconsin folklore, the Northwoods version of the Okeanos myth tells about how it was none other than the legendary lumberjack Paul Bunyan who discovered the Round River of Wisconsin. The story goes that Paul Bunyan had scouted the entire Northwoods in search of the perfect lumber camp. The one that he found was near a particularly swift river. He figured that he could pile up the downed logs along the riverbank all winter, and then, come thaw, float the haul downstream to the mill. There he set up camp and set to work with his trusty sidekicks Babe the Blue Ox and his cousin Little Benny. Sourdough Sam kept the crew fueled with flapjacks and maple syrup. After a successful winter of the crew shouting "timber!", spring came and the ice on the river opened. To prepare for the trip, Paul took off his trusty red long johns and took a bath in the always cold waters of Lake Superior. He washed and hung his long johns up to dry on a flagpole at the camp.

They set off with their winter haul heading downstream. After three days they saw signs of human life—smoke rising from the trees. When they reached the spot, they were disappointed to find that it wasn't the mill but another lumber camp—competition! The camp struck them as oddly familiar. They continued on their way. Three days later they came across another camp. This time they noticed a cook who looked just like Sourdough Sam, and some clean red long johns blowing in the breeze. "These lumber camps all look the same!", they grumbled. They continued on. Three days later they came across another camp, and again they were puzzled by how familiar it all seemed. They jumped off their rafts and confronted the cook. "Sourdough, what are you doing here?" Bunyan asked in astonishment. "I work here, and so do you!" the cook responded. "So we've been going around in a circle this whole time," the lumbering Bunyan finally concludes. They had discovered the Round River.

Of course, if you follow the trail of water far enough, all rivers eventually return, connected as part of this planet's complex hydraulic circuit. In the end, "all things merge into one," as Norman Maclean put it in his fly-fishing classic, "and a river runs through it." For Wisconsinite and founding figure of modern ecology Aldo Leopold, the Round River myth served as an ecological parable. In his retelling of it, Leopold reframes Round River as the guiding metaphor for the interdependence and interconnectedness of the biotic community, what Leopold defines broadly as "the land." Not only is there a Round River in Wisconsin, he writes, but the whole world is a Round River: "The current is the stream of energy which flows out of the soil, into plants, thence into animals, thence back into the soil, in a never-ending circuit of life." Or as the poet of Ecclesiastes so beautifully describes it: "All the rivers run into the sea; yet the sea is not full; unto the place from whence the rivers come, thither they return again" (Ecclesiastes 1:7).

The Bible tells its own Round River story. Out of Eden, the river that waters the garden flows and forks into four tributaries, watering the whole world. Throughout the Bible, these rivers trace the arc of a human lifespan, accompanying stories about source and origin as in the rivers of paradise beginning in Eden, stories about birth as in the story of baby Noah placed in a basket in the Nile, stories of young adulthood as Jesus is baptized in the Jordan, stories of mature adulthood as Jacob wrestles with his demons at the ford of the Jabbok. And finally, when we come to the end of the Bible, the world to come is imagined as a riparian paradise, with a river ("the river of the water of life") whose waters are "clear as crystal" flowing through the middle of the main street of the redeemed city of God, the new Eden; a river on whose banks stands the Tree of Life, yielding fruit for all and with leaves for the healing of the nations.

The book of Revelation is a unique text in the Bible. In terms of genre, it is the only complete apocalyptic text that we have. Apocalypse comes from a Greek word meaning "unveiling" or "uncovering," like when the curtains are pulled back in the theater to give the first glimpse of the stage setting, or when wrapping paper is torn off revealing the gift. Revelation attempts to lift the veil on the deep future, on the end of time, wrapped as it is in a dense shroud of dark enigma.

With its final unveiling, the end of Revelation offers a bright, beaming, beautiful vision of what we can call apocalyptic hope. Apocalyptic hope is a type of hope that's not necessarily dependent on present circumstances or present outlook, but that takes a deep view of time. Apocalyptic hope is the type of hope that Czech politician, dissident, and president Vaclav Havel was pointing to when he said: "Hope is not the conviction that something will turn out well but the certainty that something makes sense, regardless of how it turns out." Revelation was written at a time of great despair for the Christian community, when the Roman Empire was persecuting Christianity and otherwise seemed on a crash course to consume and conquer and burn up the world. In the face of a reality like that, apocalyptic hope trusts that, while we might not be able to see the how or when of it, the ultimate end of things will make sense and will tend towards the good because the ultimate end of things will tend towards God. The ultimate end of things will be with God. The ultimate end of things will be God.

I had apocalyptic hope on my mind as I went out one spring Friday in Vermont to support a Greta Thunberg–inspired climate rally organized by the Middlebury college, high school, and middle school students. As the crowd gathered and filled the park, holding signs like "There is no planet B," "Keep winter cold," "The world is God's Body," "You'll die of old age, we'll die of climate change," suddenly there was a chant that rose from the huddle of the young people. "We are unstoppable / another world is possible." Then the students started to give speeches, speaking from the heart about how they'd really rather not have to skip class, but that the future demanded that we take a stand and start making changes now. One young woman ended her remarks saying, "This is a battle for the dignity of our earth and everything on it—and if we don't have that, then what do we have?" The rally concluded with the students teaching us their newest protest song. "People gotta rise like water / We gotta face this crisis now / I hear the voice of my great granddaughter / Saying climate justice now."

RIVERS

I hear the voice of my great granddaughter . . .

a battle for the dignity of earth and everything on it . . .

the radical trust that "another world is possible" . . .

✳ ✳ ✳

That's apocalyptic hope. That's "Then I saw 'a new heaven and a new earth.'" That's "Then the angel showed me the river of the water of life, as clear as crystal . . .'"

✳ ✳ ✳

"Clear as crystal." That's option A on the field data sheet. A) clear; B) cloudy; C) foam; D) muddy brown; E) silty gray; F) tea; G) unnatural. Standing in muck boots in the thick clay of Vermont's Lemon Fair River early one summer morning, my only real choice was between options D and E. "What do you think?", I asked my sampling partner. "Is it muddy brown today, or silty gray?" We settled, as we usually did, on D) muddy brown. Fitting for a river that is most probably named after the French phrase for making mud, "Limon Faire," although other theories are that it's from a Yankee pronunciation of the French phrase for Vermont's Green Mountains, "les Monts Verts." Perhaps my favorite etymology is the legend that an early settler, after getting stuck in the clayplain muck, cried out "What a lamentable affair!"

I find myself standing in the muddy Lemon Fair from time to time because for the last handful of years, during the warmer months, from April through September, I've been a volunteer sampler for the Addison County River Watch Collaborative, one of a couple dozen who head out to the rivers in our area every month to collect water samples which are then sent off to a lab in Burlington, Vermont where they're tested for things like turbidity, nitrogen, E. coli, dissolved and total phosphorus. I couldn't tell you much about the science of it, but I do it because I enjoy the early morning wake-up call and invitation to go stand in a

46

river, listen to the birds, and hold a pole, which when I think about it, sounds a lot like why I enjoy fishing too. And while not a river ecologist or scientist, I've slowly found myself coming to the awareness that rivers are one of the key indicators of total ecosystem health. The health of a river is like a report card on the health of the entire watershed.

Theologian Ched Myers has developed a notion of Christian spiritual practice that he calls "watershed discipleship." By this phrase he means at least three things. One is that, as followers of Jesus who incarnated in a specific body in a specific time and place, we're always called to be Christians in a specific place as well, and since there's nowhere on this earth that isn't a part of a specific watershed, we cannot escape the fact that our Christian discipleship necessarily takes place in and is shaped by and shapes a local watershed.

Second, he uses watershed as a metaphor, like when we talk about our historical moment as a "watershed moment," as with our current climate crisis. A watershed moment is a critical moment, a tipping point. Like how one drop of rain can fall on one side of the Continental Divide and end up in the Pacific Ocean, while another can fall just over on the other side of the divide and end up in the Atlantic.

The third meaning of watershed discipleship focuses on the meaning of discipleship itself—a word that means being a student, and particularly in the Gospels, being a student of the rabbi or teacher Jesus. As Myers puts it, the earth is calling out to us today to become disciples of our watersheds, to be students of the place where we live. We need what he calls a "catechism of place."

"We won't save places we don't love," he says, quoting Senegalese environmentalist Baba Dioum. "We can't love places we don't know. And we don't know places we haven't learned."

How well, I wonder, do I know my place, my watershed? If a drop of water fell on this Vermont church roof, where would it go? What other waters would it join up with? Would they be waters of life? What trees would the waters nourish? What fish would swim in them? What insects, what plants? What song do our rivers sing? What sermons do they preach? Where would these waters begin? And where would they end? Would we swim in them? Would we as a church baptize someone in them, full immersion style, like Jesus in the Jordan? Or would the E. coli levels be too high? Would we fish and eat the fish from these rivers? And if not, should the eagle and osprey? What will these rivers look like in ten years, 100 years, 10,000 years? What do we want them to look like? What's our most beautiful, most daring apocalyptic hope for these rivers of the water of life? What's our vision of our own new Eden, our new Jerusalem, our own heaven here on earth, our own local watershed of God?

❋ ❋ ❋

This is a battle for the dignity of our earth
and everything on it—and if we don't have that,
then what do we have?

On each side of the river stood the tree of life...
and the leaves of the tree are for the healing
of the nations.

People gotta rise like water... I hear the voice
of my great granddaughter...

Then I saw "a new heaven and a new earth," for the
first heaven and the first earth had passed away...

We are unstoppable / another world is possible.

Then the angel showed me the river of the
water of life, as clear as crystal...

❋ ❋ ❋

A river meets its end when it empties into that which is larger than itself. A river returns to the great source from which it began. "The voice of the river that has emptied into the Ocean," as Sufi poet Hafiz puts it, "Now laughs and sings just like God." So too, we can hope, for the end of our own lives. But before it reaches its end, all along its way, a river is a source of life and beauty and hope as it brings things to life in such wild, profuse diversity along its tangled banks. "Wherever the river flows," the prophet Ezekiel proclaims in his vision of the heavenly river, "everything will live" (Ezekiel 47:9).

A river was there in the beginning, and a river will be there at the end. The original impulse and intention of the river's current is to bring forth and sustain the fateful and gracious ecological enmeshment of all things. Because in the end it's all a part of the sacred watershed of God. It's all a part of holiness. This garden earth of ours. This Planet A. And a river—a great Round River—runs through it.

MOUNTAINS

CREATION ELEMENT INTERLUDE: FIRE

As for the earth, out of it comes bread;
but underneath it is turned up as by fire.

—Job 28:5, "Hymn to Wisdom"

Water might have a biological claim to primacy, but from a cosmological sense, fire was first. The Big Bang theory posits that the universe began, or began its current iteration, when everything that now exists was condensed into the size of a peach pit and had a temperature of over a quadrillion degrees. The energy that was released by that fiery conflagration continues to push the universe out in an ever-accelerating expansion.

While pre-Socratic philosopher Thales of Miletus argued that water was the *arche* element, Heraclitus argued that fire was the source and origin of all that is. "The world," he wrote, "was created by neither gods nor humans, but was, is and will be eternally living fire, regularly becoming ignited and regularly becoming extinguished."

We might think first of the sun and the stars, but fire also dwells in the center of the earth. Although the earth's core is ultimately still mysterious and inaccessible, our best theory is that the core is a molten iron fire burning at approximately 12,000 degrees Fahrenheit. Wherever we move on the earth, this fire within the earth's body creates many of the essential and determinative forms of the landscape, especially when it comes to forms such as mountains. Just as I turned to rivers as one of the primary ways that the water element can speak to us, I will turn here to mountains as a way the fire element speaks to us and shapes and creates spiritual and scriptural landscape, contour, context, and meaning.

Some mountains are formed directly by fire-spewing volcanoes. Most others are made in the forge deep below the surface, as the fire in the earth's belly melts the tectonic plates at different rates depending on rock density, causing the plates to flow like lava and at times collide, converge, and well up into mountain ranges like flames that flicker and reach to the sky in jagged, forked, toothed, alpine peaks and valleys.

From a geological standpoint, mountains can be unformed just as quickly as they are formed, like Heraclitus's primordial fire that ignites and extinguishes and reignites itself constantly. Curiously, the Bible also offers an advanced geological perspective on mountains when on multiple occasions it compares mountains to candles, claiming that the mountains that seem so permanent and everlasting to our eyes can nevertheless disappear and "melt like wax" (Psalm 97; Micah 1).

Like the fire from which they are born, mountains loom on the landscape as both blessing and curse, as a manifestation of sublime beauty that in equal measure beguiles and baffles, enchants and overwhelms, compels and challenges. Moses encountered the burning bush at the foot of the mountain he would climb again and again seeking God's immediate presence. Elijah clung to his cave on the mountainside as a fire and lightning storm raged around him. In the Transfiguration, Jesus climbed to the top of Mount Tabor and shone like the brilliant fireball sun. And at the end of the Bible, the angel of God brings John up a "great high mountain" to glimpse the new Eden.

In this moment of the earth's history, God has placed us on a planet in which mountains cover one quarter of the earth's surface. Per square foot, they are home to more biodiversity than any other landscape. Mountains are also hotspots of cultural diversity. In the Himalayas, the human inhabitants speak over a thousand different languages and dialects. In addition to the impediments to travel that mountains present to land-based creatures like us, biologists theorize that this incredible density of diversity results from mountain environments hosting the greatest number of climate types and ecotones within the smallest area. Find yourself deep in midsummer's heat and craving winter's chill? A hike up a tall peak can bring you from summer to winter, with an ascent through spring's ephemeral beauty if you approach on one side of the mountain, and a descent through autumn's plaintive letting go if you descend on the other.

As microcosms of the earth and its seasons, mountains also appear to be that part of the earth that is attempting to reach beyond the earth, which speaks to the human yearning for transcendence and the beyond, the realm of heaven and the dwelling place of the gods. In his classic and comprehensive *Patterns of Comparative Religion*, Mircea Eliade includes chapters on how humans have responded to the sacred in many of the earth's basic elements and features—sun, sky, moon, water, earth, among others. Curiously, he chose not to include a chapter on mountains. My sense is that the great scholar might have felt overwhelmed in the way a novice hiker might feel as they pause at the base of a mountain they're not sure they can summit. "The symbolic and religious significance of mountains is endless," Eliade concludes with a breath of near surrender, when he finally mentions mountains near the end of his "Sky" chapter. "Every mythology has its sacred mountain," he writes, as he points to how mountains, as the meeting point of heaven and earth, appear most often in mythology and religion to represent central and centering points—the holy mountain as Axis Mundi, the center of the world. Because of "the consecrating power of height," mountains gather and focus the earth's sacred energies and desires for the divine, the sun beyond all suns.

As fire naturally rises, so too do mountains, gifting us when we follow them with long vision, and when we read them from the perspective of the sacred, they gift us with the views we most need, a glimpse of what we most long to see: creation as it is lit up by the light and warmth and ascendency of a fire—a panorama of the promised land.

I

THE THREE RULES OF MOUNTAINEERING

The knowledge of God is a mountain
steep indeed and difficult to climb.

—GREGORY OF NYSSA

Where I live there are mountains on two sides. To the west, the rugged, layered Adirondack peaks of New York. To the east, the broad, solid-sloping Green Mountains of Vermont. I turn one way and face cold, clear peaks with names like Giant, Hurricane, Upper Wolfjaw. I turn to the other and face peaks that beckon with longing and danger—Hunger, Romance, Mount Horrid.

"Look to the west," the tour guide on the *Spirit of Ethan Allen* directed us, passengers on the Lake Champlain cruise, when I first moved here. "Those are the second-most beautiful mountains in the world." We paused to take in the green-purple field of mountains beyond mountains stretching back to the horizon. "Now turn around and face the east. Those, those are the most beautiful mountains in the world."

It's hard to argue with Camel's Hump and Mansfield, although I've seen enough of this world to know that beauty is not something God tends to be frugal with.

While looking at them from afar is a lovely pastime, climbing mountains makes me nervous. On days when I plan to climb, I'll do just about anything to procrastinate. Read the maps over again. Check the weather. I'm normally relatively focused and calm. But mountains make me jittery.

The types of mountains I climb don't pose a particularly concerning physical threat. I'm not talking about K2 or the Matterhorn. I'll serenely lace up my rubber-soled wading boots for a day on the river, knowing that I could end up slipping on mossy rocks, swept downstream through boulders and rapids, putting rod and limb in peril. But when I put on my hiking boots, my heart flits and flutters. I know the feeling well because I'm feeling it now, writing early in the morning on a fine July day in which I plan to hike up Mount Abraham in Vermont's Green Mountains.

Mountains are edge experiences. They bring us to the vertical edge of this world, and perhaps also to an edge or boundary of the self. Mountains have long been thought to be where the gods dwell. When I think about climbing a mountain, especially one that takes me above timberline, I pause over this uneasy thought highlighted in Robert Macfarlane's *Mountains of the Mind: Adventures in Reaching the Summit*: for thousands of years, climbing to the tops of mountains was, in many cultures, almost unthought of or was thought to border, as he puts it, "between downright lunacy and outright blasphemy." When I find myself taking in the view from a mountaintop, there's this nagging suspicion that I might be trespassing. That I am not where I—not where mere mortals—belong.

In addition to the existential difficulty that mountains pose, there are also the physical difficulties to consider. Going up a mountain challenges the human body, puts it in abnormal positions, and strains it beyond everyday motions. It requires stamina and energy and determination. It requires you to push through discomfort and exhaustion until you reach your second, third, fourth winds. Not only do you have to lift your body upwards, pushing against gravity and the hardness of the mountain, but you have to do so while cautiously but confidently placing each foot on wobbly and erratic rock, slippery tree roots, or cold mountain streams. And in the back of your mind, you ponder the fact that every year, hundreds of people meet their end in the mountains.

If, as American philosopher William James thought, the spiritual life is defined by "the strenuous mood" that strives to test oneself and achieve that which is difficult and rare, then mountain climbing could be seen as a spiritual practice *par excellence*. The ideal peak experience becomes one only reached by passing through a great ordeal. We most fully realize ourselves on the top of a mountain when the journey there has tested us. Ascension becomes asceticism.

The climbing community summarizes the physical and spiritual difficulty that mountains pose with a maxim known as the three rules of mountaineering: "It's always farther than it looks. It's always taller than it looks. It's always harder than it looks."

When we read the Bible from the perspective of mountains, mountains are often celebrated as the beautiful dwelling place of the Divine and as awesome marvels of creation. However, we also find moments when the difficulty and challenge of mountains reveals them as sites of physical and spiritual testing, temptation, and confrontation. Mountains in the Bible can be both occasions for theophany and the intimate knowing of God, as well as occasions that reveal the immense gulf or gap in our knowledge of God. Three moments in particular stand out in this latter sense as trying, challenging moments in which the three rules of mountaineering ring true: Abraham summoned to sacrifice Isaac on Mount Moriah, Jesus tempted by the devil to rule the world while standing atop a "very high mountain," and Elijah facing earthquake, thunder, and an existential shudder while huddled in a cave on the side of Mount Horeb.

MOUNTAINS

RULE #1—"IT'S ALWAYS FARTHER THAN IT LOOKS."

Now the Lord said to Abram, "Go from your country and your kindred and your father's house to the land that I will show you."

—Genesis 12:1

Unlike Odysseus, who gives to the Western imagination the image of life as a journey that eventually leads the self back to where it began, the story of Abraham presents a different blueprint for the journey of life in which one sets off from somewhere and ends up somewhere else, a journey that doesn't lead back to the known, but pushes ever onward into the unknown. In addition to being known as the "father of faith," Abraham is also the father of all explorers—the forerunner of Roald Amundsen and Fridtjof Nansen, George Mallory and Edmund Hillary, Annie Smith Peck, Neil Armstrong, and Buzz Aldrin.

The most harrowing moment in Abraham's expedition into the unknown was when God led Abraham on a three-day journey to Mount Moriah upon which he was told to sacrifice his child Isaac.

That morning before setting out, one can only imagine a fretful Abraham splitting his firewood for the sacrificial altar and readying his donkey. With Isaac they set out on a journey towards the place God will show them. They go three days into the unknown. "On the third day," as Genesis 22:4 puts it, "Abraham looked up and saw the place far away." "Far," indeed, being an apt metaphor for the human mind trying to bridge the gap and understand the nature and way and sometimes baffling summons of God.

❋ ❋ ❋

At twenty-six miles away, if I set out on foot for Mount Abraham from my house, it might well take me three days like Abraham's journey to Moriah. "Mount Abe," as locals call it, is one of the five peaks of Vermont's "Presidential Range," and is the highest peak in Addison County.

Vermont field biologist Craig Zondag knows this mountain well. And this mountain knows Craig well. To hike it with him is to hike a mountain of stone and birdsong and lichen and moss, but also to hike a mountain of mind and body and soul and spirit. It wasn't until I hiked here with Craig that I was attentive to the moment when quartzite rock shows up on the trail; that I learned that the first major boulder deposit is a vast, angular fortress of rock called the Hall of the Mountain King; that I noticed that, after about the first quarter mile, about when the body starts to get a bit hot and sweaty on a summer day, the mountain turns cool and dark and smells of balsam, birch, and pine. "Notice how the mountain incense attaches to the open pores of the skin—I call this mountain cleansing," Craig said. The tremolo of a winter wren rang out deep in the woods, and a Swainson's thrush offered its electric melody closer by, adding to the baptismal feel of the moment.

We ascend over a stretch of the trail where the rocks lie flat like steps. Craig calls this section Jacob's Ladder. It will lead us to our destination on today's hike—not the summit with its 360-degree panorama and alpine tundra ecotone, but the moment about halfway up when the path narrows and needles through two massive boulders, one on each side of the trail.

These boulders are the Gateway to the Mountain. They are a paradigmatic "thin place" as Celtic spirituality imagines it, and as such they have a powerful effect on human mood and behavior. They direct your steps, just as the trail up the mountain directs your steps and guides your path. "Mount Abe," as Craig said, "teaches me how to walk. It teaches me how to put one foot after another. It teaches me how to find balance. It teaches me how to tread lightly, and how to move sustainably. Hiking this mountain always teaches me how to walk on the earth."

For today, we stop between these two boulders. These rocks concentrate the intention and the wisdom of the mountain. Why are you hiking here? they ask. What is your quest? The sensitive hiker must ask of this Gateway—can I proceed? Can I continue on up to the summit?

Is the peak of this sacred mountain attainable and knowable and welcoming of me?

✳ ✳ ✳

Writing under the pseudonym Johannes de silentio, Søren Kierkegaard set off on an intellectually performative pantomime of Abraham's journey to Mount Moriah, trying to imagine the depths of anxiety that the father of faith endured, the "fear and trembling" that must have accompanied him. Kierkegaard imagines many different scenarios, trying—rationally, but hopelessly in the end—to make sense of this moment and what was going through Abraham's mind. "No one was so great as Abraham," he writes, "and who is capable of understanding him? . . . In a certain sense there is nothing I can learn from him but astonishment."

As I sit on the side of Mount Abe with Craig at the Gateway, I ponder how far I would still have to go to make it to the top. Knowing that I won't make it today, I think mountain thoughts of distance and difficulty and incomprehensibility, including the impossible distance to which God pressed Abraham, who learned the mountain wisdom in the harshest way imaginable—that it's always farther than you think.

RULE #2—"IT'S ALWAYS TALLER THAN YOU THINK."

> Again, the devil took him to a very high mountain and showed him all the kingdoms of the world and their splendor . . .
>
> —Matthew 4:8

In the mountain-climbing world, there's a certain culture of "peak baggers" in which success is measured in altitude. This drive to climb the tallest and most difficult mountains is a relatively recent desire for humanity and seems to be a particularly masculine obsession to conquer and dominate nature. When Roald Amundsen reached the South Pole in 1911, the two polar blanks on the map had been filled in. Only Everest, the "Third Pole," remained.

When Tenzing Norgay and Edmund Hillary first made it to the summit of Mount Everest in 1953, their responses to the moment were illuminating. Norgay said a quiet prayer honoring Chomolungma, Tibetan Mother Goddess of the World. Hillary, by contrast, turned to British expedition partner George Lowe. "By George," he said, "we've knocked the bastard off."

Thirty years earlier, George Mallory had made three grueling expeditions to Everest. Over the course of these trips, Mallory became obsessed with conquering Everest. The first 1921 expedition was largely a reconnaissance mission. The tweed-clad group brought to the mountain tins of quail and cases of champagne. Despite the romance of the high peak, Mallory left feeling defeated by the challenge the mountain posed. In a letter from the ship on the way back to England, Mallory wrote to his sister that "I wouldn't go again next year, as the saying is, for all the gold in Arabia."

But he did go. When the second expedition team of 1922 reached the Himalayas, they had a chance to meet with Tibetan Lama Gyatrul Rinpoche before they set off for the mountain. The lama offered them tea, yogurt, and rice and asked the team what their intentions were and what they hoped would come of this trip. The lama warned them that those mountains were extremely cold and were not useful for much of anything besides meditation.

"They camped at the bottom of the mountain," he recalled in his spiritual autobiography, "and I heard that they camped seven times for each level they reached. With great effort they use magical skills with iron nails, iron chains and iron claws, with great agony, hands and feet frozen... Some left early to have limbs cut off, others stubbornly continued to climb...."

"I felt great compassion," he concluded, "for them to suffer so much for such meaningless work."

On June 8, 1924, Mallory and his climbing partner Irvine made an attempt at the summit that would be their last. In May of 1999,

George Mallory's body was finally found at an altitude of 27,000 feet. The explorer ended up as a frozen statue near the top of the mountain that obsessed and possessed him.

❋ ❋ ❋

Early in his ministry, the Spirit led Jesus into the wilderness for forty days and forty nights. The devil takes Jesus up an "exceedingly high mountain" and offers him the world if Jesus but bows down and worships him.

With a brilliant counter-parry and riposte, Jesus evokes the humble and humbling wisdom that it is God alone who is worthy of our ultimate longing and devotion, and that when we elevate anything else to that level, we do it at our own peril. With that checkmate thought, Satan is immediately discharged and defused, and angels suddenly arrive to attend to Jesus.

Jesus, it seems, in resisting the mountaintop urge to dominate and control and conquer, knew the wisdom of Lama Rinpoche's warning to peak baggers like Mallory. He knew the deep Zen wisdom of the Himalayan mountain monks, who have a mantra to help resist the temptation to claim ultimate attainment and final accomplishment: "When you get to the top of a mountain," they say, "keep climbing." For as the second lesson of the high peaks teaches, "it's always taller than you think."

RULE #3 – "IT'S ALWAYS HARDER THAN YOU THINK."

> The angel of the Lord came a second time, touched him, and said, "Get up and eat, otherwise the journey will be too much for you."
>
> —1 Kings 19:7

In 1 Kings 18, we read the story of the prophet Elijah enduring the most difficult day and night of his life. After triumphing over the prophets of Baal during a duel on Mount Carmel, and after summoning a rain cloud to end the draught that was crippling the land, Elijah, expecting a heroes' welcome, runs down Mount Carmel in glee. Shortly thereafter, though, he receives word that Queen Jezebel wants him not welcomed, but killed for his triumph. Overcome with despair, Elijah journeys alone into the desert. Falling on his knees under a broom tree, he asks God to take his life. Revived in the night by an angel of God, Elijah flees, for forty days, further into the wilderness and seeks refuge in a cave on the side of Mount Horeb. Elijah hears God's voice come to him in the mountain cave. "What are you doing here, Elijah?" God asks. The King James Version better captures it, I think: "What doest thou here?"

Come, God says, stand at the entrance of the mountain cave and look out.

The mountain throws everything that it can at the prophet. Wind rips through rock. The tectonic plates that formed the mountain rub and rumble, suggesting that just as the mountain has been made, so too it can be unmade. Elijah hears "a still small voice." He hears "the sound of sheer silence," "a thin quiet sound," as different translations put it.

Elijah wraps his face with his scarf and stands at the entrance of the cave. God's voice comes to him again. And again, God calls to the prophet with the same piercing, halting, soul-shuddering question as before: "What doest thou here?"

✳ ✳ ✳

In the summer of 1846, shortly after he was released from jail for protesting slavery, Henry David Thoreau made his own journey into the wilderness to hike Mount Katahdin deep in the Maine woods.

After a difficult trip upriver, his group reached the base of Katahdin. As the most experienced hiker in the group, Thoreau took the lead. He chose the most direct and steep path up the mountain. The few people who had reached the top before him had all taken other, less direct routes. At four o'clock in the afternoon, the rest of Thoreau's party gave up for the day. Thoreau set off for the peak alone.

At first the vegetation is so thick as to be nearly impenetrable. Thoreau had to hike straight up the path of a stream bed. He uses the word "arduous." He invokes "Satan" and "Chaos" to describe the landscape he's trying to hike up. At 1,200 feet below the Katahdin summit, dense clouds halted Thoreau's summit. He never made it to the top.

Thoreau's experience on Katahdin sent an existential shudder down his spine and shook him to his core. It unveiled an aspect of nature that he had previously neither seen nor wanted to see. On Katahdin, Thoreau met the hard, unfeeling reality of rock. Thoreau met "Matter, vast, terrific." "Perhaps I most fully realized that this was primeval, untamed, and forever untameable Nature," he wrote as he looked back on this experience.

In one of the most ecstatic prose passages in all of his writing, Thoreau describes the feeling of standing on the rock slope of the mountain and becoming newly awakened to the sheer, indifferent materiality of existence:

> I stand in awe of my body, this matter to which I am bound has become so strange to me. I fear not spirits, ghosts, of which I am one . . . but I fear bodies, I tremble to meet them. What is this Titan that has possession of me? Talk of mysteries! —Think of our life in nature,—daily to be shown matter, to come in contact with it,—trees, rocks, wind on our cheeks! The solid earth! The actual world! The common sense! Contact! Contact! Who are we? where are we?

Who are we? Where are we? What doest thou here?

After hiking back down, I linger out the afternoon with Craig at our friend Max's house at the base of Mount Abe, thinking back to how nervous and jittery I felt this morning looking ahead to hiking this broad-sloped, dark green giant that now seems like it has its back turned to me. And I make a mental note, a little prayer to my future self, that on days when I plan to hike a mountain, that something within me might remain feeling a bit uneasy. Because when you dare to approach the mountain, when you make an attempt at the summit of the world, when you reach the edge of the self, and seek the summit of God—it's always farther than it looks, it's always taller than it looks, and it's always harder than it looks.

2

THE LIVING MOUNTAIN OF GOD

Days pass and years vanish and we walk sightless among miracles.
God, fill our eyes with seeing and our minds with knowing;
let there be moments when Your Presence,
like lightning, illumines the darkness in which we walk.

—FROM THE MISHKAN T'FILAH, "A PRAYER FOR SHABBAT"

While the Nile River played a significant role in cradling baby Moses in the reeds along its banks, mountains most significantly shaped the course and direction of the prophet's life. As a young man both filled with angst over his people being subjected to indentured servitude in Egypt and filled with longing to discover his life's purpose, one day Moses ventured a bit further afield while tending to his father-in-law's flock of sheep. He made it deeper into the wilderness than ever before, all the way to the base of Mount

Horeb. Mount Horeb, also known in scripture as Mount Sinai, and known today as Jebel Musa (Arabic: "Mount Moses"), is a rugged, jagged, granite massif in the southern Sinai Peninsula that presents an impressive vertical rise (7,497 feet) from the surrounding desert floor. It's a mountain that seems designed to bask in the variegated wonders of desert light. Depending on the season and the time of day, it appears in shades of orange, red, russet, mauve, and dusty rose. While there are orchards, vineyards, and scrubby pines at the base of the mountain, the majority of the mountain itself is sheer, dry, weathered rock. It is an iconic "fierce landscape," as theologian Belden Lane terms it. "The God of Sinai," Lane writes, "is one who thrives on fierce landscapes, seemingly forcing God's people into wild and wretched climes where truth must be absolute."

On Moses's first approach to the mountain, he spots a bush that appears to be burning. Moses nears the burning bush. He marvels that the bush burns but remains unconsumed, more like a steady oil lamp than an ash-heaping brushfire. God calls to Moses from that oil-lamp bush. God stops the young man in his tracks with a call to reverence and attention. Moses takes his shoes off, for the ground he is standing on is "holy ground." God reveals the name that, in the Jewish and Christian traditions, gets about as close to pointing to the wordless mystery of the divine presence as any word or name can get. God names Godself YHWH, meaning "I am that I am," or "I will be who I will be," or "who makes that which has been made," or "who brings into existence whatever exists," as different translations put it. Being could be a close English word, or Becoming, or maybe better—being becoming itself, creation creating, existence existing, reality realizing, life living. To this day it is a common practice in Orthodox Judaism to refrain from speaking this name aloud out of reverence for the holiness that it points to and contains. And so many translate it as Hashem, "The Name."

On the side of the mountain, Hashem introduced God's self to Moses and gave the young man insight into his life's purpose—he was put here on this earth to free his people from Egypt, and to lead them back to the promised land in Israel. Excited at this high purpose calling, Moses was also hesitant when faced with the enormity of the task. How will the people trust me and follow me on this dangerous journey of liberation, he wonders aloud?

"I will be with you," God assures the young prophet, "and this shall be the sign for you that it is I who sent you: when you have brought the people out of Egypt, you shall worship God on this mountain" (Exodus 3:12).

Moses descends the mountain with his feet treading more lightly and carefully than before. Each step sends a reminder jolt up his leg of creation's holiness. His eyes are newly opened to the wonder of being itself, his astonishment at the natural world set freshly ablaze.

Many times I've gone to the mountains feeling jaded and confused by life and the world. Many times I've returned with both my sense of amazement and my sense of direction renewed. Mountains quicken our wonder and clarify our purpose.

* * *

Scottish modernist writer and poet Nan Shepherd was born (1893), lived, and died (1981) in the Scottish Highlands outside of Aberdeen, on the north side of the River Dee as it makes its way from the Cairngorm Mountains to the North Sea. The great tide and pull of her life was always in the upstream direction. She worked and studied in the Cairngorms, producing from her first-hand mountain experience a stunning literary work called *The Living Mountain* that is part memoir, part field guide, part prose-poem, part Zen Buddhist koan, part Calvinist theological inquiry into creation as the theater of God's glory.

She began work on *The Living Mountain* in the 1940s, after having published two novels and a book of poems to modest reception. When the draft of her mountain book was completed in 1945, she shared it with one friend and one publisher. These two admired the book but wondered if there would be much market for it, so it went unpublished, with Shepherd letting the manuscript rest in a drawer in her house. It wasn't until 1977, when an older Nan was going through her possessions, that she picked up the manuscript and gave it another look. In the meantime, she had never stopped exploring the Cairngorms. When she read it again, more than thirty years after writing it, she "realized that the tale of my traffic with a mountain is as valid today as it was then. That it was a traffic of love is sufficiently clear; but love pursued with fervour is one of the roads to knowledge."

The book was published in 1977 and has since become a classic of nature literature, calling for a place next to John Muir, Peter Matthiessen, Mary Oliver, and Rachel Carson. In 2016, the Royal Bank of Scotland graced their new £5 note with a portrait of Nan and two of her quotes. The first was from her 1928 novel *The Quarry Wood:* "It's a grand thing, to get leave to live." The second was from *Living Mountain:* "But the struggle between frost and the force in running water is not quickly over. The battle fluctuates, and at the point of fluctuation between the motion in water and the immobility of frost, strange and beautiful forms are evolved."

Nan Shepherd's approach to writing in *The Living Mountain* reflects her approach to hiking. "At first," she writes, as a young woman, "mad to recover the tang of height, I made always for the summits, and would not take time to explore the recesses." *The Living Mountain* tells the story about how, over time, her approach to "hill-walking" developed and matured beyond the fixation with altitude and peaks.

In *The Living Mountain*, rather than making out for the summits, Nan explores the mountains more aimlessly, with serendipity and curiosity leading the way as she wanders deep into the recesses, the plateaus, the lakes and streams of the hills. For her, the pilgrim's method of circumambulation, peregrination, Kora, replaces the mountaineer's technical, competitive, linear summit fever. "Often the mountain gives itself most completely," she writes, "when I have no destination, when I reach nowhere in particular, but have gone out merely to be with the mountain as one visits a friend with no intention but to be with him."

For her, the body's senses, not the trail, lead the way. She compares her hiking method to that of a dog sniffing around and following wherever the scent might lead. Indeed, among other sensory accounts, she reports on the different smells of the mountain: "Pines, like heather, yield their fragrance to the sun's heat . . . the bog myrtle . . . is cool and clean, and like the wild thyme it gives its scent most strongly when crushed . . . juniper is secretive with its scent . . . and Birch needs rain to release its odour. It is a scent with body to it, fruity like old brandy, and on a wet warm day, one can be as good as drunk with it."

The Living Mountain is structured like a creation narrative. There are twelve chapters, evoking the wholeness of a year's journey around the sun. Her account of the mountains begins at the basic level with what she calls "the elementals"—rock, water, ice, air, sun. It continues with the softer, creaturely life in the mountains—plants, birds, animals, insects, humans. The final movement is a poetic meditation on the senses and the ways the mind and the mountain interpenetrate to give a final picture of the mountain as a living whole—"the mountain's wholeness," she calls it, "one entity, the living mountain."

❊ ❊ ❊

Moses took God's invitation to worship Hashem on that mountain seriously, and three months later, after trial and danger, after plagues and battles and the Red Sea parting, he led the people out of Egypt and through the wilderness, back to Jebel Musa where they were able to set up a safe and remote base camp and pause for a bit to regroup. Moses, eager to be back on the "holy ground" of his burning-bush theophany experience, eager, as we all ever are, to have an immediate encounter with the divine, immediately sets off on his first ascent up the mountain to meet God, holding fast to his first-hand, empirically based belief that Hashem lives on that specific mountain. This is no small thing. God, for Moses at the time, had a specific and clear address. Not in the trees or clouds or rivers. But in the mountains. And not on any mountain, but on Mount Sinai.

This extended stay at the holy mountain is in many ways the foundational moment in the Hebrew Bible—it's when the Israelites receive the Torah and the Ten Commandments. It's the touchstone moment that is recounted every year on the Shavuot holiday. Later rabbinical interpretation posits that every soul that would ever be born was present there at Mount Sinai to receive God's teaching and God's covenant, and that in fact we're all still in some sense there, camping at the base of the mountain, awaiting a word from the Lord. To go to synagogue or to go to church is to sit there at the base of God's mountain and to discuss and discern amongst ourselves how to interpret the revelation that comes down from on high—what it means, how to live in relation to God, one another, and God's creation.

On the first ascent, "Moses went up to God," as the scripture puts it, and "the Lord called to him from the mountain" (Exodus 19:3). God has a message for Moses to bring back to the people. Remember this moment, God says. Remember how God granted liberation from bondage. Remember how "I bore you on eagles' wings and brought you to myself," God says. If you keep covenant with me, God promises, then you shall be a "holy nation."

Moses hikes down to relay this mountain message, starting a back-and-forth conversation with Moses, the mountain, God, and the people that would continue for the next year, as Moses went back up and down the mountain at least eight times. Like Nan Shepherd returning again and again to the Cairngorms, creating The Living Mountain out of her "traffic of love" with the mountains, Moses enacts his own "traffic" with Mount Sinai, one which resulted in the Laws of Moses, the Torah, and the Ten Commandments. Moses returned to the mountain again and again, learning it in every season and under every aspect of light, approaching the mountain as a way of growing in knowledge and understanding of God, the very mystery and materiality of being itself—of being becoming, of reality realizing itself. Rather than climb many mountains, rather than "bag" many peaks, rather than casting a broad net in his explorations, Moses went in and up and deep on one single mountain. As naturalist Richard Nelson has put it, "There may be more to learn by climbing the same mountain a hundred times than by climbing a hundred different mountains."

In hiking up and down Mount Sinai again and again, Moses is the mediator between God and the people. And on the way up, and on the way down, Moses soaks in the wisdom of the mountain. The mountain wisdom guides his steps, as he learns the routes by which the mountain will allow him safe access and safe departure. The mountain wisdom seeps through his pores as he sweats under the heat of the sun and returns to him when he drinks from the crisp mountain streams. The mountain wisdom guides him by the nose, as sagebrush mingles with clay dust in the heat of the day, and juniper sweetens and sharpens the cool hours. "Each of the senses," as Nan Shepherd knew well, "is a way in to what the mountain has to give."

On the morning of Moses's fourth ascent, there is thunder and lightning. A thick dark cloud covers the mountain. The people gather at the foot of the mountain, fearing for Moses as he begins to ascend under such ominous conditions. They hear a loud blast that sounds like a trumpet. They smell smoke coming up off the mountain. Moses ascends and disappears into a cloud of thick darkness.

Mystics like Gregory of Nyssa and Pseudo-Dionysius have seen in Moses's ascent a trail map for the soul's ascent to God—the notion that one gets closer to God the higher up the mountain one goes, and that at the top, the ultimate encounter with the divine happens under the thick, dense darkness of cloud. The thought is that bewilderment and wordless wonder, not clarity and certainty, grow as we move closer to the absolute mystery of God. The final moment of encounter is beyond understanding. "The divine is there," Gregory of Nyssa writes about Moses on the mountain, "where understanding does not reach."

"Knowledge does not dispel mystery," as Nan Shepherd puts it, but deepens it. The more she visited, and the more she learned from the mountain, the more her sense of the mountain's unknown and unknowable aspects grew, too. "One never quite knows the mountain," she writes on the first page of *The Living Mountain*. "However often I walk on them, these hills hold astonishment for me. There is no getting accustomed to them."

"Knowing another" she writes on the last page, "is endless . . . The thing to be known grows with the knowing."

* * *

In chapter ten ("Sleep") of *The Living Mountain*, Nan Shepherd describes perhaps the most curious of her hill-climbing practices—taking naps and sleeping on the mountains as a way of learning them. "No one knows the mountain completely," she writes, "who has not slept on it." She calls this spiritual practice "quiescence." "One neither thinks," she continues, "nor desires, nor remembers, but dwells in pure intimacy with the tangible world . . . Those moments of perceptiveness before sleep are among the most rewarding of the day. I am emptied of preoccupation, there is nothing between me and the earth and sky."

Nan's practice of mountain quiescence is akin to meditation or prayer. It's a method for emptying the mind. For making the mind like a mountain lake, mirroring reality. "For falling asleep on the mountain," she writes, "has the delicious corollary of awaking. To come up out of the blank of sleep and open one's eyes on scaur and gully, wondering, because one had forgotten where one was, is to recapture some pristine amazement not often savoured."

I imagine Moses on the mountain during his sixth ascent, sleeping and waking on the mountain for forty days and forty nights. On the top of my closest mountain here in Vermont, Snake Mountain, I have a practice of closing my eyes for a few minutes on top of the mountain. In meditation, I let the thoughts of the day rise to consciousness and drift away on the ever-present wind on the summit. They glide away like the hawks, vultures, and ravens that play in the mountain air currents. I try to forget for a moment everything I think I know about life and the world. I draw as close as I can to a place of still blankness, to that cloud of thick darkness that Moses knew—the gracious void, the generative absence from which all things arise.

And then I open my eyes. With a good dose of "pristine amazement," the first thing I notice is the physical, material reality of the world. There's rock; there's sky; there's cloud and sun and field and a lake that shines like lapis lazuli tiles. There's all this muchness when there might just as well have been nothing. Radical amazement only begins to capture the feeling. If I stick with this first feeling, I notice that I too am part of all this—body, mind and spirit—and that body, mind and spirit—full being aliveness—is pervasive everywhere and in everything that I see. Reality is a single, interrelated blanket-like field, and it's all alive and changing and moving—my body with its movements of heartbeat, vision, hearing, touch, thought; the clouds with their perpetual drift; the wind dancing with the wildflowers and trees; the midday light fading into evening into dusk into night into dawn into day again; everything appearing, changing, disappearing, appearing again. Everything is moving all the time, without beginning, without end. YHWH, Moses heard when he opened his eyes and saw the burning bush—God identifying God's self with the vast, endless unfolding of existence—Being becoming itself.

✸ ✸ ✸

When Moses descends after being away for those forty days, he is dismayed to find that his people have started to turn from their worship of God, and instead have fashioned a golden calf and are worshiping this idol. In a fit of rage, Moses smashes the two stone tablets upon which are written the Ten Commandments. The God of the mountain is angered too, and thunder and lightning, fire and smoke make the mountain tremble. Moses makes a quick seventh trip up to plead with God to forgive his "stiff-necked" people. God only partway relents and lets go of the anger and disappointment.

Moses knows the conversation isn't finished yet, and so he prepares himself for his eighth and final ascent up the mountain. God tells him to bring two new stone tablets and to rendezvous on the mountain early in the morning. No one else is to come with Moses this time or even watch him ascend. Even the animals are to be kept from grazing at the base of the mountain.

On top of the mountain, holding his two blank tablets, Moses is visited by God, again in a cloud. God stands next to Moses and speaks again the name that Moses heard at the bush—YHWH. God passes by Moses as swiftly as the summit wind and whispers to him truths about God's nature. Truths about God being "merciful and gracious," "abounding in steadfast love and faithfulness." Moses, overcome by the power of the moment, "quickly bowed his head to the earth, and worshiped" (Exodus 34:8).

Speechless, Moses came down from Mount Sinai for the eighth and final time, carrying the two tablets with him again, fresh with the ink of God's hand, timeless instructions for living life in its fullness and rightness and beauty. And the people were amazed, because when the prophet came down off the mountain this final time, after this immediate encounter with God, his face was shining, glowing with the glow of God.

There's a striking photograph of Nan Shepherd that has her glowing in the mountains too. The photo shows her standing contrapposto, barefoot and alone in a field of wildflowers. She's wearing a long white linen shirt-dress, the bottom tattered by the rocks and wind. In one hand she holds a walking stick. In the other, a field guide, or a chapbook of poetry. A canvas satchel holds supplies for her day wandering in the Cairngorms. She's near the top of the plateau and looking downhill at the exact same angle as the mountain, with a gentle but playful smile that she would have described with one of her favorite words that recurs as a central theme in her work—*fey*, the Scots term for "bodily lightness" and "joyous release." Her face is like a mountain pond, reflecting and glowing with the warm daisy hue of the soft, hazy summer sky.

In the last chapter of *The Living Mountain*, "Being," Nan Shepherd reflects on her journey of gradual awareness and awakening towards realizing the mountain as an integral whole—as a representation and metaphor of creation's essential oneness. That the mountain is not just the peak but the rivers and the air and the wildflowers and the animals and the people and the sky and the valley and on and on. The "total mountain," she calls it. "Slowly I have found my way in . . . It is an experience that grows; undistinguished days add their part, and now and then, unpredictable and unforgettable, come the hours when heaven and earth fall away and one sees a new creation. The many details—a stroke here, a stroke there—come for a moment into perfect focus, and one can read at last the word that has been from the beginning."

I think about Moses on that eighth descent bringing back the second copy of the Ten Commandments. I imagine that on the mountain he too had one of those moments of clarity—a vision of the total, integral, interconnected mountains-and-rivers-and-valleys world of God. A vision in which everything belongs and has its place. A moment of empty mind mirroring existence in its fullness and glory. A moment in which Moses could "read at last the word that has been from the beginning." And so, Moses wrote down the words that he heard in that timeless Word and he carried them back down to his people, a gift from the living mountain of God. A gift of the spiritual opportunity and invitation not to seek to dispel but to seek to deepen the mystery of existence. Moses called it YHWH. In the last words of *The Living Mountain*, Nan Shepherd called it Being. "To know Being," she writes in the last sentence, "is the final grace accorded from the mountain." Mystery deepened, Being graced, Wonder peaked. These are a few among the many blessings of the mountain.

3

THINKING LIKE A MOUNTAIN
(A CLIMBING HISTORY OF CHRIST)

*In Louisville, at the corner of Fourth and Walnut, in the center
of the shopping district, I was suddenly overwhelmed with the
realization that I loved all those people, that they were mine and
I theirs, that we could not be alien to one another even though
we were total strangers. It was like waking from a dream of sep-
arateness . . . And if only everybody could realize this! But it
cannot be explained. There is no way of telling people that they
are all walking around shining like the sun.*

—THOMAS MERTON, *CONJECTURES OF A GUILTY BYSTANDER*

In reading the Gospels, we find that journeying with Jesus is largely
an outdoor affair, with so many of his encounters and teaching taking place by rivers, lakes, fields, hills, deserts, gardens, and public
squares. And whether he's off praying by himself, or teaching, healing,
or feeding large crowds, Jesus seems to have had a particular fondness
for mountains. Like Moses and Elijah before him, Jesus found himself

decidedly in the Hebrew mountain prophet tradition. Matthew's Gospel in particular is clearly mapped by mountains. Scholars posit that the structure of the narrative—the key features of the map—are the seven mountain stories Matthew uses to tell the journey of Jesus's life.

Jesus's ministry begins when Satan drives him to the wilderness to test him for forty days and forty nights. At the culmination of that season of testing, Satan leads Jesus up "a very high mountain" (Matthew 4), tempting Jesus with the panoramic view from the top, telling him that he can have it all, the whole world, if he just bows down and gives his soul to the devil. As I recounted in "The Three Rules of Mountaineering," Jesus responds that God alone is worthy of our ultimate devotion, and immediately, the devil disappears, and angels appear and care for him. In the next chapter, Jesus gathers a crowd, hikes up a mountainside, and sits down to teach, offering his life's keynote address, his greatest mountain sermon, the Beatitudes and the Sermon on the Mount. Later on, in Matthew 14, when he needs a break from all the action, Jesus steps away by himself, and hikes a mountain to pray, a regular spiritual practice of his that all the Gospels make reference to. Refreshed and re-inspired, in Matthew 15 Jesus once again gathers a crowd and hikes up a mountain with them. This time rather than teaching, he offers healing and he feeds the multitudes. Two chapters later Jesus's journey reaches a hinge point. The story is about to shift from Jesus's teaching and healing in the Galilee region to his final journey to Jerusalem. At this turning point, all three synoptic Gospels place the most stunning of all the mountain moments in the climbing history of Christ—the Transfiguration atop Mount Tabor.

* * *

Jesus took with him Peter and James and his brother John and led them up a high mountain, by themselves.

—Matthew 17:1

I imagine there's a certain eagerness and excitement in the air. The four friends are grateful for this time apart that they have with one another—for this change of scenery and for this change of pace. They're grateful to get to soak in the presence of one another in this small group setting, as Jesus's mountain time is often either a solitary affair or a large group gathering. They journey to the base of the mountain that rises about six miles southeast of Jesus's hometown of Nazareth. Mount Tabor, a striking cone-shaped monadnock, rises to an elevation of 1,843 feet, looking taller than it actually is against the flat, fertile landscape of the Jezreel Valley. It's the closest mountain worth climbing to where Jesus grew up. In Luke's Gospel it's referred to simply as "the mountain" (Luke 9:28) with something of the unspoken familiarity with which locals refer to their frequented landmarks— "the beach," "the river," "the woods."

They pause at the trailhead to look up at the mountain rising in front of them. The peak seems to be just out of view behind the sloping ridge. They talk about how long the hike might take—three hours, four maybe? They reminisce about the last time they went hiking together. Then they each look down, making sure their leather sandals are strapped on tightly. They look up again, this time at the sky. It's a nice day. A blue sky with a few delicate high cirrus clouds. The weather shouldn't be a problem. It's a good day for a hike. One last look towards the top, one last adjustment to their sandals, and they're off.

I imagine that their initial adrenaline takes them a good way up the mountain before they make their first stop, pausing to catch a second wind. Perhaps they haven't been talking much on this first leg of the hike, as each has been trying to keep up with the person in front of him, as each has been trying to settle into the rhythms of the hike.

When they pause, though, they savor the chance to talk amongst themselves. They want to know about the trip they're about to take in a few days to Jerusalem, the trip that will eventually lead to Jesus's imprisonment and execution. Why are we going, they ask? What are we going to do there? Where are we going to stay? What if something happens to you? Are you sure about this?

"Look," he says, as he points to a caterpillar that they had almost stepped on, just preparing to make its own metamorphosis or trans-figuration. "Look," he says, and points to the rare Mount Tabor lark-spur, a vibrant blue-flowering perennial grass. "Listen," he says, as they pause to take in the energetic, scratchy, sweet-marbled song of the Sardinian warbler.

Suddenly they start to remember what Jesus taught them on a pre-vious mountain excursion, to "look at the birds of the air," and to "con-sider the lilies of the field." The birds and the flowers are always completely themselves, and always completely in the moment. They find life and beauty without worrying about the future, but simply by resting and trusting in the grace of God.

They all pause a bit longer and look out at the world together— the sparrow landing on the pine branch, then taking off; the wind mak-ing the forest sing and sway for a moment, before leaving behind only silence and stillness; and in the distance, cloud shadows drifting across fields of almond and barley.

They set off again, this time intent on making the summit. The rest of the hike up I imagine them becoming more and more in-step with the rhythms of the mountain, with the rhythms of the hike, with the rhythms of the conversation, such that by the time they reach the peak, they've become fully attuned to the moment, merged with occurrence. And then, in something like the state of having their atten-tion restored to maximum capacity, they finally see what's right in front of them, and what's been right in front of them the whole time.

And he was transfigured before them, and his face shone like the sun, and his clothes became dazzling white.

—Matthew 17:2

"The glory of God," wrote the second-century theologian Irenaeus about this moment, "is a human being fully alive."

On the top of the mountain—suspended somewhere between land and sky, between heaven and earth—Jesus, Peter, James, and John find themselves completely exposed, open to the elements and to one another, and it's as if they realize and marvel at the fact that there's really nobody else for them to be but themselves, there's really nowhere else for them to be but in the moment, and when the disciples look at Jesus through these clear eyes of attention they finally see him for who he really is. "When they opened their eyes and looked around," as Matthew 17:8 (The Message) puts it, "all they saw was Jesus, only Jesus."

They see Jesus in a way that they never had before. They see Jesus for who he most truly is, a human being fully alive, the glory of God. And like each of us when we're seen for who we are by another, Jesus glows with that sense of recognition. Jesus glows for having been seen. Sunlight pours from his face.

※ ※ ※

Each moment fades into the next, and when you hike to the top of a mountain, the time will come when you have to turn around and hike back down, back to the world again. Such "peak moments" don't last forever, but they can linger forever like spots of time that leave a lasting imprint on the scroll of the spirit.

For Jesus, Peter, James, and John, "back to the world" in this case meant back to the journey of preaching and teaching and healing that would eventually cause such a stir with the powers-that-be as to have Jesus arrested and executed. It meant regrouping for their next and last big climb together, up to Jerusalem and to all that was waiting for them there.

I imagine they hike down with the lightness and playfulness of the body working with and not against gravity. They reach the place where they paused on the way up. They pause again to take in one last view of the expansive perspective on the world that being on a mountain affords. Despite the exertion of the hike, they feel stronger than they felt on the first pause. They feel less anxious about the future. They feel more attuned to their bodies, and to the body of the earth. The mountain has had a tonic and healing effect.

They have been to the mountaintop, and now, like Bodhisattvas who have made it to the gates of nirvana, they feel the call to turn back and return to the world, and to take up their part in the sacred work of repairing the world, and of bringing peace and justice to the suffering and dispossessed.

* * *

The hinge point in the climbing history of Christ is the moment of transfiguration atop Mount Tabor. It's the moment of truth that sheds light on all the other moments. Hebrew folk etymology connects Tabor (רובת) with *tabbur* (טַבּוּר), meaning navel. Mount Tabor, then, as a great belly button of the world, an axis mundi around which everything else finds its place and meaning, a still point in this turning world.

When we are well poised and steady, we talk about "being like a mountain." Aldo Leopold called it "thinking like a mountain." He tells the story of his ecological awakening to the interconnectedness and inter-dependency of the whole community of being he once experienced on a mountain in New Mexico. When he was a young natural resources manager, his group was assigned the task of exterminating the wolf pop-ulation. In addition to complaints from ranchers, the thinking at the time was that fewer wolves would equal greater numbers of deer and so would be a boon for the hunting community. "In those days," Leopold writes, "we had never heard of passing up a chance to kill a wolf." On one such hunt, he heard the howl of a wolf echo in the mountains and sensed that such a wild cry held a meaning that was beyond his understanding, "a deeper meaning known only to the mountain itself. Only the mountain has lived long enough to listen objectively to the howl of a wolf."

His group got within range and fired away liberally and indiscriminately, as was their way. "We reached the old wolf in time to watch a fierce green fire dying in her eyes," he writes. It was a moment of epiphany for the young naturalist. He realized his ecological thinking had been woefully shortsighted and anthropocentric. He needed to radically expand his sense of the ecological whole and the belonging of everything. He needed to start learning how to "think like a mountain," with their long, steady, expansive view of how everything has its place in the family of things.

Jesus, it seems, had this mountain wisdom all along. Jesus knew how to think like a mountain, or perhaps better, he knew how to think with the mountain, or how to let the mountain think through him. He tapped into the ecological and ethical wisdom of the mountains when he preached the radical message to "love your enemies." He said we should strive to relate to one another and to this world as God does. God "makes the sun rise on the evil and the good," he taught, "and sends rain on the righteous and the unrighteous" (Matthew 5:45). In other words, be like a mountain, Jesus teaches. Be like a mountain that remains unfazed by whatever befalls it, be it sun, rain, wind, snow. The mountain accepts and receives it all.

❊ ❊ ❊

He climbed a mountain and invited those he wanted with him. They climbed together.

—Mark 3:13 (The Message)

When Jesus arrives in Jerusalem on the week of the Passover, he chooses the Mount of Olives as his staging grounds for his time in the city. It's from this mountain that he rides a donkey into the city, cheered on by shouts of hallelujah and waves of palms. It's from the Mount of Olives that he offers his last teachings and prophecies, known as the Olivet

Discourse (Matthew 24–28). He peers into the deep future and offers his most extensive apocalyptic vision. He teaches that we can't know exactly when or how the day of God will arrive, but that we must remain vigilant to witness it. He teaches prayerful attention to what God is doing in the moment, just as he taught from the Mount of Beatitudes. He offers perhaps his most radical ethical teaching—that however we treat "the least of these," we treat him. From this mountain, Jesus looks out over Jerusalem and weeps over this world he so dearly loves. From the garden at the base of this mountain, Jesus prays to God on the night of his arrest. After his death and resurrection, Jesus invites his disciples to join him one last time, again on the Mount of Olives. There he speaks his last words to them, known as the Great Commission. "Go out and train everyone you meet, far and near, in this way of life," he says. "I'll be with you as you do this, day after day after day, right up to the end of the age" (Matthew 28:19–20, The Message). And then from the top of the mountain, Jesus ascends into heaven.

To follow Jesus on this journey of discipleship is to be one of his climbing companions. Come to the mountains with me, Christ summons, and I'll show you the wisdom of earth and the revelation of heaven. I'll show you the still point, the center, the belly button of the world. Come climb with me, and I'll show you the wisdom of the mountain, and the healing energies of the mountain. Climb with me, and your ecological consciousness will grow large like a mountain, and your attention will grow sharp like the mountain eagle's cry, and you will recognize and be recognized, you'll see and be seen, and the world will come fully alive and you will come fully alive. Sunlight will pour from your face.

4

PANORAMA OF THE PROMISED LAND

Now away we go towards the top.
Many still, small voices are calling "Come Higher."

—JOHN MUIR

When you reach the five-car-limit parking lot on the winding, gravel Route Sixty-Six in Waltham, Vermont, you've found the right spot. Exiting your vehicle, you might have to walk up and down the road a bit to find the trailhead. It's unmarked and hidden behind a bramble of highbush cranberry and goldenrod. It looks like little more than a deer path, of which there are a few in the area that might lead you astray. About thirty yards into the trail, the path widens under a canopy of hardwoods—maple, beech, poplar. The entrance proper is marked by a green and gold sign tacked to one of the white pines at the base. Alerting the hiker that they are entering private property, the owners of the Buck Mountain trailhead welcome you to enter this mountain with care and reverence. "We consider this forest a sanctuary," they write, "and expect all who enter to treat it with respect."

With that word "sanctuary" slowing my steps and measuring my thoughts, I continue up a path that has become a favorite hike of mine over the last years. "Hike" is perhaps too strong a word for it, as Buck Mountain is quite a modest peak at 883 feet. I think of Buck Mountain as a younger sibling to Snake Mountain to the south and Mount Philo to the north as the Taconic range splinters through the Champlain Valley. "Saunter," is perhaps a more apt word for the way I like to move up and down Buck Mountain, recalling John Muir (himself recalling Thoreau's essay "Walking"), as Muir compares sauntering and hiking, and playfully derives a folk etymology for "saunter":

> Hiking—I don't like either the word or the thing. People ought to saunter in the mountains—not hike! Do you know the origin of that word "saunter"? It's a beautiful word. Away back in the Middle Ages people used to go on pilgrimages to the Holy Land, and when people in the villages through which they passed asked where they were going, they would reply, "A la sainte terre," "To the Holy Land." And so they became known as sainte-terre-ers or saunterers. Now these mountains are our Holy Land, and we ought to saunter through them reverently, not "hike" through them.

"A la sainte terre," "To the Holy Land"—a wonderful mantra, I think, for any journey out the door and into the world, and perhaps especially for exploring mountains. From the Biblical perspective, at least—from Moses's view of the Promised Land from Mount Nebo, to the mythical longing for Mount Zion, to the final revelation of a new heaven and a new earth being established as a city on a high mountain (Revelation 21)—there's a clear connection between paradise and mountaintops, and a clear conviction that the world to come, the world perfected and made whole at the end of time, will be a mountaintop world. "God's holy mountain, beautiful in elevation," as the psalmist dreams of it, "is the joy of all the earth" (Psalm 48:1).

✳ ✳ ✳

Moses was 120 years old when he climbed his last mountain. At the end of his forty-year wilderness expedition, nearing the land where God had promised to bring his people, God leads Moses up to the top of Mount Nebo:

> Then Moses went up from the plains of Moab to Mount Nebo, to the top of Pisgah, which is opposite Jericho, and the Lord showed him the whole land: Gilead as far as Dan, all Naphtali, the land of Ephraim and Manasseh, all the land of Judah as far as the Western Sea, the Negeb, and the Plain—that is, the valley of Jericho, the city of palm trees—as far as Zoar. The Lord said to him, "This is the land of which I swore to Abraham, to Isaac, and to Jacob, saying, 'I will give it to your descendants'; I have let you see it with your eyes, but you shall not cross over there." Then Moses, the servant of the Lord, died there in the land of Moab, at the Lord's command. He was buried in a valley in the land of Moab, opposite Beth-peor, but no one knows his burial place to this day. Moses was one hundred twenty years old when he died; his sight was unimpaired and his vigor had not abated. The Israelites wept for Moses in the plains of Moab thirty days; then the period of mourning for Moses was ended.
>
> —Deuteronomy 34:1–8

This is one of the most poignant, thin-veil-type moments in scripture. After his years of wandering and leading his people, Moses is granted a view of the Promised Land, but not entrance into that land himself. He gets close enough to see it, to lay his eyes on it, but not to step foot on it, not to touch the dirt, not to smell the grass, not to taste the water. Moses on Mount Nebo speaks to the limits of our reach in this life and to the limits of our longing. Moses on Mount Nebo speaks to how we're here on this earth for a finite time, which means that our deepest dreams and hopes, which are imbued with a sense of the infinite, the perfect, the complete, will remain incomplete and unfulfilled. Moses on Mount Nebo reveals that what we most long for lies just on the other side of what we're able to accomplish in this life.

"The secret to life," as sculptor Henry Moore put it, "is to have a task, something you devote your entire life to, something you bring everything to, every minute of the day for your whole life. And the most important thing is—it must be something you cannot possibly do!" The journey to the Promised Land, which was the journey to freedom, which was the journey to God, was that task for Moses. Second-century Rabbi Tarfon put it similarly: "It is not up to you to finish the work of perfecting the world, but neither are you free to avoid it." *Tikkun olam* is the Jewish ethic that develops from this perspective—from Moses on Mount Nebo, getting close enough to see paradise, but not reaching it. "Repair of the world," it translates.

✳ ✳ ✳

About halfway up the saunter to Buck Mountain, there is a small side trail on the east that leads you to a beaver pond. With that word "sanctuary" still guiding my steps, I consider a pause at this pond to be an essential part of the Buck Mountain climb. The pond lies on the side of the mountain as a sort of Inner Sanctum, with the thrum of bullfrogs as the choir, the raft of wood ducks and mallards as the congregation, and the one-legged, solitary sandpiper as the odd officiant. Turtles lounge on the fallen logs and cedar waxwings circle around the dead tree trunks standing in the still water. Dragonflies chase each other while a tiger swallowtail butterfly flits its way around the pond's edge. It's a wonderful service, and the sermon is among the best I've heard. In the distance, the deep throaty kraa of a raven marks the benediction and speaks of the heights and the view from the mountaintop that is to come.

Once back on the trail, the mountain starts to make itself known as you climb over the first ledges of exposed bedrock. Granite and quartzite mingle from the ancient bedrock of time. The trail gently rises over the course of a few switchbacks covered in ferns and moss. Playful squirrels and chickadees make cheerful the way. After one last sweep as the trail ushers you along the side of the exposed mountain rock, you turn the last corner and come to the summit, bright and refreshing like a lake of sky seen through the leafy trees. Emerging from the edge of the tree line feels like a curtain is being pulled back: a panoramic, postcard view opens before you. Hawks, vultures, and ravens glide overhead, sending their shadows swooping on the exposed cliff edge; the head of Snake Mountain stares back at you and connects to Buck Mountain through a low-ridged continuous forest, a wildlife corridor separated on either side by two patchwork quilts of field and forest. To the east, a newly constructed solar array shimmers like a glassy pond, seeming in some ways more natural and liquid than the metal roof on the barn to the west that glares in the sun like a signal flare.

I stand for a moment, thinking about Moses reaching the top of Mount Nebo. He had just offered his final words—known as "the Blessing of Moses"—to his people. "May God bless you," he said as he left them for his final mountain climb, "with the choicest gifts of the ancient mountains; and the fruitfulness of the everlasting hills" (Deuteronomy 33:15). Having blessed them this last time, he left the group and hiked up Mount Nebo alone.

I imagine the view opening up before him as he reached the summit. Mount Nebo rises in western Jordan to a height of 2,740 feet, although its perch seems higher as it looks down on the Dead Sea, 1,385 feet below sea level. Across the Dead Sea, Moses would have looked out at a sweeping landscape, taking in the Jordan River valley, with towns like Jericho and Bethlehem, and, on a clear day, Jerusalem in the distance. God offered Moses a view of his heart's deepest longing—a panorama of the Promised Land. I imagine Moses lingering with that view for a while, not wanting to leave it. And perhaps he never did. Moses breathed his last breaths somewhere on or near Mount Nebo. In the fourth century, a monastery was built on the mountain to commemorate his view of the Promised Land and to mark his grave.

Instead of the Dead Sea, I look out on Lake Champlain. In place of Bethlehem and Jericho, I look out on Addison, Bridport, and Weybridge, and on a clear day, Middlebury and Middlebury College shine at the base of the Green Mountains. Buck Mountain is one that I always bring my binoculars to. Without them, the Weybridge Congregational Church steeple disappears into the trees. With them, the slender white spire rises to its humble perch on the side of a wooded hill. About the same size as the trees, the white steeple looks like a lone birch surrounded by a circle of maples. Focusing my binoculars on the steeple from Buck Mountain today near the end of August, I verge on tears of joy and gratitude as I enter my last week of pastoring this church that will always have a special place for me as my first call. Unlike Moses, who was granted a panoramic view of the Promised Land that he would see but not enter, I gaze from Buck Mountain today on a panoramic view of the actual landscape where I've lived and labored. I look out on the roads I've crisscrossed; the homes I've visited; the rivers I've fished and paddled; the hills I've sauntered and hiked; the cemetery where I've buried people; the sanctuary where I've preached. This church community, with its Open and Affirming, Creation Justice ethos, and this landscape, with its stunning beauty, have been the inspiration and in many ways the coauthors of this writing project. The trees, the clouds, the rivers, the mountains—it's all here, all part of the whole, the glory of the world that I've been eager to— and prayed to be worthy of—reporting on.

Among the many allures of mountains, the panoramic view from the top holds a special appeal. Panorama comes from the Greek roots pan (all, total) and horama (sight, spectacle, that which is seen). It means something like "the view of the all," "the total-view," "the whole-view," "all-embracing," "comprehensive," "entire," "complete." From the tops of mountains, we look down on a world that is both the world that we know and at the same time like a map of the world that we know. We can see how the world fits together, where things are in relation to one another—we can see how all things are related, connected. Mountains offer us a glimpse of the Whole, the All—where all things belong and the beauty of God shines through. "Out of Zion," the psalmist writes, again dreaming of that holy mountain of the world-to-come, "the perfection of beauty, God shines forth" (Psalm 50:2).

I linger out the afternoon on the top of Buck Mountain, sitting on the summit, trying to take in the panoramic whole. Cloud shadows drift over the back of Snake Mountain. A farm truck labors under the weight of its carry, leaving a rising line of dust like the contrail of the airplane that moves overhead towards Montreal. A scarlet tanager zips across the summit, a sudden streak of red against the blue and white sky.

For a moment, everything feels in its proper perspective. Everything belongs and everything belongs to everything else. The way everything seems to fit together when viewed from above, it makes sense that when the Biblical imagination envisions the world made perfect, it pictures a mountaintop scene. Known in scripture as "Mount Zion," "God's holy mountain," "the new Jerusalem," "the mountain of the Lord's temple," the Bible sees in mountains a glimpse of the more beautiful world that is to come, the future justice, the future glory. At the very end of the Bible, an angel of God leads John "to a mountain great and high" (Revelation 21:10), to see the new heaven and the new earth and gives the Bible its benediction—God shall be with the people and God will wipe away their tears and weeping and mourning and death shall be no more.

MOUNTAINS

If you want to see paradise, the Bible seems to say at the end, go climb a mountain and look out, and shining through the landscape of this world, you just might glimpse it—everything fitting together—perfection perfected for a moment—a panorama of the Promised Land—this earth as the sanctuary, as the holy land, as la sainte terre, that it is.

TREES

CREATION ELEMENT INTERLUDE: EARTH

The earth is the very quintessence of the human condition.

—HANNAH ARENDT

I f the universe began with fire, and if biotic life began with water, then creaturely life, including human life, could be said to begin with earth. In the creation myth of Genesis 2, God forms *adam* from the *adamah*, the human from the humus. We homo sapiens, who dream soaring soul dreams, were made from the soil of the earth, and when we die, the earth will receive us by dissolving our mineral bones back into its fold. Dust to dust, ashes to ashes, earth to earth. We are, as the prophet Jeremiah imagines it, clay in the potter's hands. We are, as the apostle Paul puts it, earthen vessels. To be human is to be an expression of earth in its bipedal journeying, willful shaping, and self-reflective wondering.

From the garden in Genesis to the new earth in Revelation, the earth element undergirds the whole sweep of the Bible. The story, for Christians, begins with the adam figure and ends with the Christ figure, whom Paul addresses with the title Last Adam, Second Adam, or Ultimate Adam (*eschatos adam* in Greek—see 1 Corinthians 15:45). Although Jesus had a powerful affinity with all the elements—able to calm wind, able to walk on water, able to baptize with fire—it is the earth element that features most prominently in his teachings and parables, and in many of his ritual actions, such as using clay to heal a blind man's eyes and inviting the disciples to his eucharistic feast where he identifies his body with the earth element of bread from the field.

In his parables, we often find Jesus drawing on earthy images to teach us about the nature and mystery of God. He spoke about seeds falling on thin soil and on rich soil; he used mustard seeds and fig trees as his sermon illustrations; he marveled at the lilies in bloom. He was born on a farm and compared people to lost sheep. He called humans the salt of the earth. He pictured the kingdom of God as a woman baking bread and on the sabbath he walked through the fields foraging for ripe grains of wheat that he would pop into his mouth. He was, as the Gospel of John imagines it, the clearest indication of the incarnation, of the word of God made flesh, of the God expression translated into the earth element.

"The kingdom of God," as Jesus taught, "is as if someone would scatter seed on the ground, and would sleep and rise night and day, and the seed would sprout and grow, he does not know how. The earth produces of itself, first the stalk, then the head, then the full grain in the head" (Mark 4:26–28). "The earth produces of itself," Jesus says— the earth produces *automatos*, as the Greek puts it, self-prompted, self-sufficient, requiring no external effort, spontaneous and self-propelled. The kingdom of God, Jesus says, is like this: it just happens, it percolates, it rises up on its own, the way the dandelions in spring sprout up everywhere without anyone having planted them. "The rose is without why," as the seventeenth-century German mystic Angelus Silesius put it, "it blooms simply because it blooms."

If we think of the earth as the landscape against which or within which our lives unfold, it seems to have a Zen-like presence—at once a solid composure and a playful spontaneity. The earth has been here longer than we have, and so the earth is our witness, having watched us arrive. How curious we must seem to the earth, which is always there— or here, rather—and fully present and centered in itself in a focused but calm and generative way, whereas we humans are haunted by notions of elsewhere and beyond and are driven to stressful and destructive frenzy by our struggle to be present like the earth is and to be as accepting of things as they are and where they are and why they are.

If air and fire are upward moving elements, then water and earth are downward moving. We connect to the earth by sending our energy down our spines to our legs and our feet as they touch the ground. We sink into our identities by connecting with our ancestral roots, just as a tree grows by sending its roots downward. When feeling healthy and good, we say we feel grounded.

The earth element is the heaviest and densest element and is ruled by gravity. In our bodies, we experience gravity as a downward pull. But when we think of the planet as a whole,* and when we imagine the activity of gravity from a whole earth perspective, we see that gravity is not a downward pull but rather an inward pull, drawing matter from all sides towards the earth's core. Gravity, as the power of the earth element, is an inward pull towards the center of things, towards essence.

Perhaps this energy towards the center accounts for the Zen-like presence of earth as landscape. We humans set off on extra-planetary excursions seeking who knows what, meanwhile the rose blooms

---

*Earth, curiously, is the only planet not named after a Greek or Roman god, but instead is named for what it most immediately is, namely ground, dirt, soil.

without why, the earth produces automatically, spontaneously, and the lilies of the field are filled to the brim with all the beauty that exists without ever having a thought or worry for the past or the future. "A tree," as Thomas Merton put it, capturing something of the earth's self-composed enlightenment, "gives glory to God by being a tree."

In Genesis 2, immediately after God forms adam from the adamah, God forms trees, a glorious expression of the earth element. With roots that draw water, they reach towards the fire ball sun, and on their way, they alchemize the air element, turning carbon dioxide into oxygen. Although trees and plants existed for hundreds of millions of years before humans, Genesis is right to intuit that our stories are fatefully entwined. Trees and plants rule the earth—accounting for eighty percent of its biomass—turning planet Earth into a solar powered garden of life. Human flourishing goes hand in hand with, and is directly dependent upon, botanical flourishing.

The Bible begins with the Tree of Knowledge and ends with the Tree of Life, and with more references to trees than to any other aspect of creation besides humans, trees loom like an old growth forest over the tangled undergrowth of scripture. Perhaps this is because trees are the earth element in its most generative, most sublime design and expression. Perhaps this is because we've long understood that trees have what we long for: patience, longevity, generativity, abundance, community and kinship, resilience.

Trees give glory to God by being fully themselves, and by being fully present to whatever season of life they find themselves in. Every spring they model the most surprising of resurrections and every fall they model the most beautiful of mortalities. To be blessed, to be happy, to be enlightened, as Psalm 1 imagines it, is to be like a tree planted by streams of water. We fellow earthlings and clay creatures might do well to rest from our restless wanderings, bow to the earth element, and look to the trees.

I

TREES AND BEAUTY
ECOLOGICAL ETHICS AS AESTHETICS

*The more clearly we can focus our attention
on the wonders and realities of the universe about us,
the less taste we shall have for destruction.*

—Rachel Carson

Trees appear on the first and last pages of the Bible. Other than God and humans, trees are the most mentioned living thing in scripture. You'll find trees present at many of the key turning points in the drama. If you're looking for significant landmarks to guide your path through the tangled bank of scripture, look for the blazes on tree trunks like you would on a hiking trail.

When we begin reflecting on the theme of trees in the Bible, it is only fitting that we would begin at the beginning, starting with the opening verses of Genesis as they tell their poetic version of what remains a largely mysterious and unknown and astonishing story—the story about how all of this came to be. After moving past the murky and impossible questions about the first moments—why there is something rather than nothing, light and darkness, space and stars and planets—the next big question is, how could something as beautiful and as fragile as life emerge from such seemingly lifeless or inanimate elements?

A scientist might teach here about how plants and trees fundamentally altered the earth's atmosphere by dramatically decreasing carbon dioxide levels and dramatically increasing oxygen levels, which in turn made it possible for life to take on so many other forms. Or about how green things figured out how to capture the energy from the sun and make it available here on earth—because of plants and trees, life lives by eating sunshine. From a more theological perspective, it's interesting to pause in Genesis 1 on the third day of creation, the day that plants and trees were created, and to ponder a bit about what the text says about that moment.

> And God said, "Let the waters under the sky be gathered together into one place, and let the dry land appear." And it was so. God called the dry land Earth, and the waters that were gathered together he called Seas. And God saw that it was good. Then God said, "Let the earth put forth vegetation: plants yielding seed, and fruit trees of every kind on earth that bear fruit with the seed in it." And it was so. The earth brought forth vegetation: plants yielding seed of every kind, and trees of every kind bearing fruit with the seed in it. And God saw that it was good. And there was evening and there was morning, the third day.
>
> —Genesis 1:9–13

The third day is unique in at least a couple of ways. On most other days God steps back at the end of the day and pronounces creation "good." Here God pronounces creation "good" twice. The third day is the only day to receive this double blessing. There is power, the writers of scripture seem to be suggesting, in the number three. In Jewish numerology, one symbolizes unity, agreement, simplicity. On the first day of creation, according to Genesis, life as such hadn't been created yet. There was only God. Day one, in a sense, was a day of one, of unity, of completion. The number two symbolizes separation, dichotomy, and tension. On the second day, God separates the waters above (heaven) from below (earth), creating a basic duality. The second day, interestingly, is the only day not pronounced "good." The number three is the number of harmony that includes and brings together the two opposites. On the third day, God set the opposites working together in order to create life—plants and trees. The third day doesn't undo or fix the separation of the second day, but it brings the opposites together to be part of a greater whole. And it's this third day, the day when the duality is transcended and made generative, that is pronounced doubly good. This power of "the third day" is a recurring motif in scripture. Jonah spends three days in the belly of the great fish. Jesus spends three days in the tomb before resurrection. And Jesus's first miracle—turning water into wine at the wedding feast in Cana—was said to have occurred "on the third day" (John 2:1). This is why some traditional Jewish families continue to hold weddings on the third day, on Tuesday, the day of trees, the day of double blessing.

Thinking about trees, God's blessing, and weddings, I cannot help but think about one of the most memorable weddings that I was honored to be a part of. In July 2016, I officiated at my sister Hannah's wedding to my brother-in-law Johnny. They chose to have a rustic, outdoor wedding on our family's cabin property in northern Wisconsin. The year before, a couple of oak trees had fallen on the property. They cut the trees in half lengthwise to make ceremony benches on the hillside sloping down towards the lake. They molded their rings out of twigs from the property. When they exchanged those rings, the three of us plus their wedding party were all standing on pine needles, as the tallest white pine on the property, my family's favorite tree, smiled down on us. The day before we had cleaned up the fish bones the bald eagles would often leave at the base of the tree, it being one of their favorite perches on the lake. And so, that day all we could smell was the clean, heady, precise perfume of the pine. The wedding was on a Saturday, not a Tuesday, but the sense of double blessing was palpable. As I preached and pronounced my blessing upon the couple, I knew that the wind in the pine needles was offering another sermon and another blessing. While we were both preaching, a great blue heron and two eagles flew by behind us. Sometimes life really is that beautiful. Blessing upon blessing.

The Eastern white pine (*Pinus strobus*) holds a special place in my spiritual imagination. It's the tallest tree in the landscape of my soul, being the tallest tree east of the Mississippi, where I have always lived. Sometimes referred to as "the Sequoia of the East," the white pine can reach heights of over 200 feet. Something in the way the white pine stands tall and proud and dark speaks of all things north, and wild, and free. Although I've seen it many times, one of the most beautiful sights I ever expect to see in this life is a bald eagle perched in a white pine. The ink-black body with the painted-white head and tail, framed by a pine-green deep enough with the pigment of life to withstand even the coldest of winters—it excites sight in a similar way to how the fragrance of pine excites smell. I can easily imagine God stepping back and having to do a double take—pronouncing the white pine good and then good again.

※ ※ ※

Another unique aspect to the third day in Genesis is that God makes a subtle change to God's method of creating. On the first two days of creation, God directly calls the thing in question into being—let there be light, and there is light; let there be a dome in the midst of the waters, and there is a dome in the midst of the waters. It is a decidedly top-down way of creating. On the third day though, God doesn't actually create plants and trees directly, top-down, but calls on the earth itself to bring forth plants and trees: "Then God said, let the earth bring forth vegetation ... and the earth brought forth vegetation." It may be a subtle change, but I get the sense here that with plants and with trees, God is inviting the earth to be a co-creator, to be a partner in the process of creation, and that from this point on, creation and creativity won't only be a top-down affair, but something that can rise up from below.

Interestingly, Genesis 1 says much the same thing when it comes to the creation of humanity on day six. Biblical scholars have pointed out a symmetry built into the first six days of creation. The first six days consist of two cycles of three days, wherein each day of the first three parallels each day of the second three. On day one, God creates light and on day four, God further fashions that light into sun and moon and stars. On day two, God separates the waters from earth and heaven, and on day five, God continues to work in the realm of water and air, creating fish and birds. On day three, as we've seen, God creates the plants and trees, and invites the earth to be a generative co-creator with God. On day six, God further works on the earth, creating animals and humans, and calling on us to "be fruitful and multiply." And although God doesn't exactly pronounce a double blessing on the sixth day, God does magnify the common blessing refrain. God looks over everything and declares it not just good, but "very good."

With this parallel structure connecting days three and six, the first creation account in Genesis suggests a deep kinship between trees and humans, a foundation for the major presence of trees throughout the Bible. Trees, in some sense, are the models, the prototypes of living beings working with God, as partners in creation. It's the same task God honors us with.

I ponder this deep mythical partnership as I ponder my family's favorite white pine on the edge of the lake. One of about a half dozen or so large pines on this stretch of shoreline, I imagine if I had been standing here two hundred years ago there would have been hundreds of white pines in view, and some that towered about twice as high as the tall pine that we so love. Before the arrival of Europeans, white pines were the undisputed kings and queens of the eastern forest, and when the newcomers first saw them—their size and their number—they couldn't believe what they took to be their good fortune. The British Royal Navy, the largest in the world, was running out of options for ship masts. They had long ago used up (that is, cut down) all their local resources, and were having to import mast trees from Russia, Norway, and Bosnia. The white pine made for the tallest, strongest, lightest mast that the European naval world had yet seen. Acting as if he had dominion over the forests of "New England," King George I declared ownership over all the tall white pines, and his soldiers traveled around branding them with a three-pronged symbol known as "The King's Broad Arrow." This action started to brew early resentment in the American colonies, such that almost two years before the Boston Tea Party, there was an equally contentious rebellion in New Hampshire as the colonists rebelled against the crown over the rights to the tall white pines. The Pine Tree Riot of 1772 was an early and significant rebellion against British control of the colonies and a major impetus for the American Revolution, so much so that the pine was the earliest symbol of colonial resistance and was used as an emblem on flags and currency. The first flag of the American Revolution, for example, the Tree Flag, is a white pine with the words "An Appeal to Heaven" written above it. A similar pine flag flew at the Battle of Bunker Hill in 1775—a red flag with a white square in the upper left with a green pine tree outline. Over the course of the next century, the white pine would play an even more significant role in the development of the United States, as the westward expansion was largely spurred by the early country's insatiable desire to build with soft, strong, light, tall pine.

Northern Wisconsin where I'm writing was at the heart of this logging-based development of the country, as the vast stands of pines were cut down and shipped, first by river, and then by train, south to Chicago and beyond. Today, less than one percent of the white pine east of the Mississippi that the European settlers found when they arrived here remains. And in Wisconsin, which was a logging capital, the number of old pines is even fewer. Wisconsin naturalist John Bates estimates that of Wisconsin's sixteen million acres of forest, less than 0.2% are more than 150 years old. The area is still heavily wooded and deserving of its moniker of the "Northwoods," drawing thousands of tourists with the beauty of its forests. Most of these woods, however, are young second growth, and many of them were planted by the Civilian Conservation Corps in the 1930s. By then, the logging industry had worked over the entire northern part of the state. The CCC stepped in to plant new forests, in part because the clearcut landscape with fields of stumps and charred remains was incredibly barren and hauntingly ugly for the year-round residents. Wisconsin continues to be a leading logging state today, although the days of mass clearcutting seem behind us, with more sustainable forestry practices emerging. Living in a landscape so defined by trees and so shaped by the history of our interaction with trees, it's not hard to feel the wisdom of the ecological ethic implied in day three and day six of the Genesis 1 account—our relationship and our similarity to trees speaks to the heart of our call to be co-creators with God, and co-stewards, of this adventure of life on planet Earth.

※ ※ ※

That there are two different stories of creation in the first chapters of Genesis has long puzzled readers. The first seems to take a more distant and cosmic vision. It sets out an orderly account of God fashioning one aspect of creation after another like a master artist or engineer would, whereas the second story in chapter two is a more down-to-earth story, a messier story with more room for imperfection. It is told less from the cosmic perspective and more from the (at times all too) human perspective. It tells the story of humanity as Adam and Eve in the Garden of Eden and of our fateful exile from the garden paradise. While different in almost every way from the first story of creation in

Genesis 1, trees appear in both stories as prominent characters and play pivotal roles in the drama.

One immediate difference in the second story is that rather than being created many "days" or millions of years before humans, humans were created right before plants and trees were created. Or maybe it's better to say that we were all created in the same moment—that when God made us out of the dirt of the ground, God took the same ground and made trees and plants and the entire garden scene for us to live in:

> In the day that the Lord God made the earth and the heavens, when no plant of the field was yet in the earth and no herb of the field had yet sprung up—for the Lord God had not caused it to rain upon the earth, and there was no one to till the ground; but a stream would rise from the earth, and water the whole face of the ground—then the Lord God formed man from the dust of the ground, and breathed into his nostrils the breath of life; and the man became a living being. And the Lord God planted a garden in Eden, in the east; and there he put the man whom he had formed. Out of the ground the Lord God made to grow every tree that is pleasant to the sight and good for food, the tree of life also in the midst of the garden, and the tree of the knowledge of good and evil.
>
> —Genesis 2:4b–9

Before any other creatures were created, when God thought about the natural environment for us to live in, the first thing God thought of was trees—that if there's going to be humans, then in some deep ecological sense, what they'll need first is trees to live near. This lines up with one of the leading theories of human evolution, which asserts that our earliest ancestors lived near and likely up in trees.

Another interesting thing to ponder here: the text tells us that humans and trees are made out of the same stuff, out of the ground or the dirt of the earth, which again is scientifically or literally true, and for many human cultures has been symbolically or mythically true as well. As a consequence, it tells us that part of our fascination with trees lies in the many striking similarities that we can see and sense between ourselves and trees. Trees are like us in that they have a bone-like, skeletal structure; they have bark like we have skin, and like us their skin shows marks of stress and age and bleeds sap like we bleed blood; like us but unlike almost any other creature, trees stand tall and upright against the horizon; like us they go through seasonal changes; like us their bodies are made up of mostly water; they have a crown of leaves like we have a crown of hair, and in old age for both of us that crown might start to thin. It makes basic biological sense then, that from the perspective of our earliest religious or spiritual awareness, trees seemed to symbolize life itself, as in the Tree of Life that Genesis mentions and that so many other myths from around the world also mention, from Yggdrasil in Scandinavian myth to Grandmother Cedar in Ojibwe myth. Trees map our most basic cosmological awareness and orientation by directly participating in the three basic realms of life that we sense: their roots reaching down to the underworld and the dead, their trunks planted firmly in this world and in this life, and their branches and leaves reaching up to the heavens and the afterlife and to the realm of the gods.

It's not surprising, then, that the Tree of Life is one of the first two trees that are mentioned in Genesis 2. What's more surprising and unique to the Biblical imagination is the other tree that's named and that plays a pivotal role—the fateful Tree of the Knowledge of Good and Evil. This is the only tree that God tells Adam and Eve not to eat from, and so of course, being human and insatiably curious, they cannot help but reach out and try it, opening the first rift in creation, the first moment when we become aware of our distance or separation from God, and so the first moment when we become exiled from paradise.

I'm afraid far too much ink has already been spilled on this one moment in the Bible, and the interpretations range from the harmful and misogynistic ones that seem to forget that little detail in our text about how Adam was standing right next to Eve when she grabbed the fruit, and about how Adam ate it with her without protest, to other interpretations that celebrate Eve here as a Promethean hero of humanity who simply acted out of our best human impulses to gain knowledge and understanding of the world, which is an interpretation that continues in our technological era with the Apple logo (an apple with a bite out of it), designed to honor Eve's daring action.

When we read the story from an ecological perspective, we might find that that one tree also has something to teach us about how we should and shouldn't relate to all trees, and by extension to all of creation, and by extension to God.

Here's one hypothesis about what this moment in scripture might have to teach, and it comes from a little detail in the text. The moment when trees appear in this story reads, again, "Out of the ground God made to grow every tree that is pleasant to the sight and good for food."

I wonder if the order in which God describes the purpose of trees here isn't significant. The first thing God says about trees is that they were made to be pleasant to the sight—that they were made simply to be beautiful and for us to admire and appreciate them for their beauty. Only secondarily does God say that they are also made to be good for food, that they can also be useful to us in some direct, material way. Interesting, particularly because when Eve goes on to describe the tree, she does, in fact, reverse the order, "When the woman saw that the tree was good for food, and that it was a delight to the eyes . . . she took and ate."

It's as if God said that the first thing you need to notice about trees is that they are beautiful. If and only if you notice that first, then you might be able to eat their fruit, then you might be able to use them for your benefit. And then it's as if God gave us a little test to see if we got the point. God said you can eat from all of the trees but this one.

In other words, you'll have plenty to eat, more than enough. But if eating—if consuming—is the only way you know how to relate to things, then you are taking a fateful step in the wrong direction.

✳ ✳ ✳

Although only 0.2 percent of the old forest survived the nineteenth-century logging campaign, you can still find pockets of old growth that hold trees that were alive long before the first Europeans set foot in the Northwoods. While not as famous as the stand of old growth pines and hemlocks in the northeastern corner of Wisconsin aptly named the Cathedral Pines, the closest community of old pines near our cabin is in the Drummond Woods in Bayfield County. Now preserved as part of the Chequamegon-Nicolet National Forest, the area was once owned by the Rust-Owen Lumber Company. Signs of the lumber history abound along the short, three-quarters of a mile interpretative trail that is a side loop connected to the North Country Scenic Trail. Relics of the lumber era remain. You'll find cast iron tools half buried and old railroad ties covered in moss underfoot along the trail, as this area has been set aside with the purpose of being an "outdoor history class," as one of the initial signposts describes it. The interpretative trail tries to take a balanced moral approach, honoring the logging history and its influence on the economy and culture of the Northwoods, while also honoring the old pines and hemlocks that were spared during the major logging period.

Winding through a mixed forest of yellow and paper birch, basswood, sugar and red maple, the trail eventually circles a tamarack marsh, the delicate needles a glowing honey cream yellow as the seasons turn in late October when I visited. Eventually you come to the stump of a massive pine called King Pine, marking the entrance into the heart of the old grove. Struck by lightning twice, King Pine died, they say, in 1978. With snow covering its base, and green moss covering the top, the stump looks alive still in some way. Hollow in the center, it looks like a telescope that the earth is using to gaze out at the heavens. It would have been over 300 years old.

Soon you'll find a gathering of white pines as large around as the King Pine, and an extended family of hemlocks nearly as big. With not much growing in the understory, and with the tall trees giving each other ample elbow room, the grove feels expansive, spacious, and cavernous compared to the tight and snarled thicket of younger forest that surrounds it. The trunks impress first. Rather than feeling settled and having a downward energy as you might expect, the trunks of old white pines have an upward and uplifting energy, as if the earth were gladly and with great confidence and strength reaching up, like a giant's hand wearing the earth as a glove and sleeve.

Also impressive is their ability to grow vertically straight even while on a slope, standing as if with a clear conscience, as Thoreau intuited when he wrote that "nothing stands up more free from blame than a pine tree." Commenting on the logging of the old pines in Maine, Thoreau lamented the loss of "the living spirit of the tree" to the lesser purpose of lumber. The pines, he wrote, are "as immortal as I am, and perchance will go to as high a heaven, there to tower above me still." Standing in the old grove, with the sense of coherent, contained space, solid, ascending presence, incensed smell, the celestial sound of wind in pine needles, and the way sunlight tinsels and shows its joy in the white pine boughs, it is clear beyond doubt that there is spiritual value inherent in old forests. In some ways it feels like a world apart from the woods that I am familiar with, the messier, denser, more impatient adolescent forests that are the norm here. In another sense, being in an old forest has the feeling of coming home.

The Drummond Woods was set aside by the lumber company in the 1880s, when the employees requested that some of the beautiful old pines be saved for their families to enjoy and recreate in. Although we might wish there were more than 0.2 percent left, I am grateful that at least some of our ancestors heard the whisper from Genesis, that first and foremost trees are beautiful, and that beauty is their primary and ultimate purpose. Only after appreciating their inherent beauty might we then learn how to use them wisely, and maybe learn that wisdom sometimes means not using them at all.

I take one last look at the old pines and hemlocks in the Drummond Woods. I thank them for sharing their beauty with the world for these past centuries. I ask forgiveness for the ways we've reversed the order of ecological ethics that we find in Genesis 2:9. I pray for a world wherein the beauty of what is leads us to act in wisdom. "Let the beauty we love," as poet Rumi put it, "be what we do."

I drive back to the cabin through a seemingly endless stretch of younger forest. While still sorting themselves out, the trees are impressive in their diversity and vigor—birch, pine, oak, maple, aspen. It's a feast for the eyes. I look to one side of the road and see that it is good. I look to the other, and see that it too is good. The trees remind me that we live in a world that is more than blessed—that is filled with blessing upon blessing.

2

ABRAHAM AND SARAH ON HOSPITALITY
PRACTICING OAK ETHICS

I like to look at a tree and see that it's love. Don't you?

—RAM DASS

ost scholars locate Abraham in Mesopotamia during the Middle Bronze Age, sometime between 2100 and 1900 BCE. Around this time, the wooly mammoths took their last breaths and humans in Turkey were beginning to experiment with smelting iron. In central Iran, a Mediterranean cypress that you can visit today was already a couple of hundred years old—planted, according to legend, by the prophet Zoroaster. The Cypress of Abarkuk flourished when Abraham walked the earth, and it continues to stand verdant and strong today, estimated at 5,000 years old. It is but one of the many thousands-years-old plus trees that we find alive today. Perhaps the oldest is Old Tjikko, a sixteen-foot spruce that set its roots almost 10,000 years ago on Fulufjället Mountain in northern Sweden.

In Fishlake National Forest in southern Utah, there is a clonal colony of 40,000 quaking aspen, all connected by a single root system that has been replicating and regenerating its stand for the last 80,000 years. Pando (Latin for "I spread") is also known as the "trembling giant" on account of the unique way that aspen leaves can photosynthesize on both sides, making them quicker than most leaves to dance in the wind. Pando is the oldest living organism on planet Earth.

What's going on here, we might wonder? How do trees get to be so old? The answer, according to recent research such as the work of German forester Peter Wohlleben, has to do with how profoundly socially interconnected trees are. In *The Hidden Life of Trees*, Wohlleben documents the myriad ways in which the flourishing of individual trees is directly tied to the flourishing of the forest community. Parent and grandparent trees, for example, have a curious pedagogical method for raising their young. One would think that the more sunlight a tree gets the better off it will be, but tree parents raise their young by way of strategic light deprivation. Developing at a slower rate leads, in the long run, to healthier, older, more resilient trees. And at the end of a tree's life, the direction of care flows back, as younger trees send nutrients to dying and even apparently dead tree stumps for hundreds of years after the old tree can provide for itself.

In the undisturbed beech forests that Wohlleben studied, he found that rather than maximizing individual energy production, a community of trees tends to synchronize their rates of photosynthesis and growing performance. This leads to a community in which all individuals are equally successful, regardless of the arbitrary start they each received due to the particular soil composition, elevation, and sun exposure where the tree took root. The forest, it seems, creates its own social safety net, privileging the wellbeing of the whole over the self-interest of the one. This is the essence of forest wisdom. On their own, a tree is completely subject to external weather conditions. Together, a forest can create its own climate, moderating extremes of heat, cold, wet, dry. The old saying is radically (to the roots) true: "A tree can only be as strong as the forest that surrounds it."

✳ ✳ ✳

Three of the world's major religious traditions (Judaism, Christianity, and Islam) trace their roots back to Abraham. As the only person in scripture described as a "friend of God," Abraham is still looked to as a paragon of faith. Where, we might wonder, did Abraham learn such intimacy with God? Where did he learn the wisdom of faith as a primary existential relation to the world, such that thousands of years hence, we still find ourselves as branches and leaves on Abraham's still-living tree?

What if we read Abraham's story from the perspective of trees? Almost immediately, when God started appearing to Abraham these appearances tended to happen in the presence of trees. Following God's call to wander into an unknown land, Abraham finds himself pausing under "the oak of Moreh" (Genesis 12:6). It was here that God appeared to Abraham and declared that this land would be for his ancestors. Abraham had entered his holy land, the landscape of his soul, and its entrance was marked by a tree (perhaps echoing how the guarded and hidden Tree of Life had marked the expulsion from Eden). Abraham built his first altar to God under that oak tree. In Genesis 13, God calls Abraham to explore this new landscape—"northward and southward and eastward and westward" (Genesis 13:14). Abraham sets off exploring and finally sets up a more permanent camp under the "oaks of Mamre." Likely in a rural spot in the West Bank desert, the oaks of Mamre would prove to be the favorite campsite of Abraham and Sarah. After further wanderings, they would return here in Genesis 18, where God would appear to Abraham again, and in perhaps the most dramatic and theologically decisive way of his life:

> The Lord appeared to Abraham by the oaks of Mamre, as he sat at the entrance of his tent in the heat of the day. He looked up

and saw three men standing near him. When he saw them, he ran from the tent entrance to meet them, and bowed down to the ground. He said, "My lord, if I find favor with you, do not pass by your servant. Let a little water be brought, and wash your feet, and rest yourselves under the tree. Let me bring a little bread, that you may refresh yourselves, and after that you may pass on—since you have come to your servant." So they said, "Do as you have said." And Abraham hastened into the tent to Sarah, and said, "Make ready quickly three measures of choice flour, knead it, and make cakes." Abraham ran to the herd, and took a calf, tender and good, and gave it to the servant, who hastened to prepare it. Then he took curds and milk and the calf that he had prepared, and set it before them; and he stood by them under the tree while they ate.

They said to him, "Where is your wife Sarah?" And he said, "There, in the tent." Then one said, "I will surely return to you in due season, and your wife Sarah shall have a son." And Sarah was listening at the tent entrance behind him.

—Genesis 18:1–10

This is the foundational Biblical text on hospitality. In a sense, this story is told again and again throughout the Bible, making hospitality one of the grand themes and threads of scripture. Jesus references this story in his own teaching on hospitality: "I was a stranger and you welcomed me" (Matthew 25:35). The Letter to the Hebrews in the New Testament gives us a poetic and concise interpretation: "Do not neglect to show hospitality to strangers, for by doing that some have entertained angels without knowing it" (Hebrews 13:2). The Quran thinks so highly of this story that it retells it three different times.

Abraham is resting in the shade of the oak trees in the heat of the day. He is enjoying the microclimate that communities of trees can create. The Talmud claims that when the strangers arrived, Abraham was talking with God. He was deep in private prayer. But when they arrived, he stopped the conversation and offered them hospitality. This shows, the Talmud argues, that extending hospitality to the stranger is even more important than our private conversations with God. Or perhaps we might think of it this way: extending hospitality to the stranger is the conversation God is always eager to be having with us.

Abraham is on the lookout for travelers passing by. He doesn't wait for them to ask if he has a glass of water to quench their thirst. Instead, he goes to them—he runs—and invites them to share the cool of the oak trees. "Let me get you a little bit of water," he says, "and let me bring a little bread, while you rest yourselves here under the tree."

That turns out to be a quite an understatement, as Sarah uses at least three days' worth of the finest grade of flour to bake her best bread, while Abraham prepares the choicest calf and provides the best dairy that he has access to. "Just a little water and just a little bread," he had said, before spreading out before his visitors this lavish field-to-table feast, all set under the cooling shade of those oak trees. One ancient rabbi tried to explain Abraham's understatement here by noting that when it comes to hospitality, the righteous ones speak little, but do much.

We might wonder, since this is indeed the first moment of extravagant hospitality that's described in the Bible, where or how did Abraham and Sarah learn to extend such a generous welcome to others? Of course, one traditional answer has been to locate this story within the anthropological context of the practices of the nomadic, desert Bedouin culture. "The ancient law of the desert," as it's known, teaches that in such a harsh landscape, a social contract to practice hospitality is a matter of life and death. On any journey, one could find oneself as the thirsty, hungry, tired wanderer dependent on the generosity of others to survive the night. And for those providing the hospitality in a landscape in which visitors could be few and far between, the chance to host is the chance to connect with the outside world and learn the news of the day. Outside visitors allow the hosts to remember and retell the story of who they are and so to keep the ember of their identity glowing. More often than not, hospitality proves to be a mutual gift. The three strangers receive an extravagant welcome, some cooling shade, and a gourmet meal, but Sarah and Abraham receive a gift of inestimable value—a promise that even in their old age they will be blessed with a child. They realize the full theological truth of hospitality—that in welcoming strangers, they in fact welcomed God into their midst without even knowing it. In offering food and rest, they learned the ethical wisdom that the other person's material needs are my spiritual needs.

As helpful as the "ancient law of the desert" theory is in interpreting this text, there seems to be something more going on here than mere survival. The reason this text has developed into such a strong, deep root is that the hospitality Abraham and Sarah show truly is extravagant. They go above and beyond. They go the extra mile. Again, we might wonder—where did they learn the wisdom of such extravagant hospitality?

I think about those oak trees that they so loved to camp beneath. What might Abraham and Sarah have learned from living in such close proximity to those trees, the oaks of Mamre? Waking up to the sound of birdsong in the canopy. Laughing at the squirrels tousling in the branches and stashing away acorns for future use. Marveling at the timeless mystery of how something so small as an acorn could turn into something so grand and majestic as a mature oak. Watching at dusk as other animals like deer and turkey come to feed off the abundant mast.

From an ecological perspective, trees are masters of hospitality, creating the conditions for thousands of other species to flourish. If you picked up a handful of soil from the forest floor and counted up all the little beings, there would be more life forms in that handful of soil than there are humans on the planet. But even within the tree world, no species has mastered hospitality quite like the oak tree.

Oak trees are a classic example of a keystone species—one species upon which many species in the ecosystem directly depend. Every oak forest is its own biodiversity hot spot. Valley oaks in California, for example, have been documented to support 300 animal species, 1,100 plants, 370 fungi, 716 lichens, and 5,000 insect and invertebrate species. An oak hosts 534 species of caterpillars. By comparison, a gingko tree, common to plant in urban areas, hosts five species. A chestnut hosts four. This diversity quickly extrapolates and magnifies itself. It takes 6,000 caterpillars to raise one brood of chickadees. So birds love oaks too, as do all the other creatures you might find in an oak forest: deer, bear, rabbit, raccoon, flying squirrels, chipmunks, woodpeckers, wood ducks, wild turkeys, jays, magpies, hummingbirds, and even us humans—oak being an essential provider of food (three days' work of gathering acorns is enough to provide hunter-gatherer communities with a years' worth of flour), shelter, and heat. In the much-loved children's book by Shel Silverstein, the "Giving Tree" was an apple tree. An ecologist would take issue with this. In truth, the real "giving tree," the forest master of hospitality, would have to be an oak.

✳ ✳ ✳

Genesis 18:1 begins a special portion of the Torah called the *Vayeira*—the Appearance. It is named after the first word—אַרְיַן—"And appeared . . ." *Vayeira* comes from the root "to see." The full sentence reads, close to literally: "And appeared (or, And brought-about-being-seen) to him (Abraham) YHWH in the oaks of Mamre." Traditionally, this opening sentence is read as a type of dramatic irony—a case in which the reader knows more than the characters in the drama do. In this case, the reader knows that the three visitors are actually God or God's messengers in disguise. But when we linger with that opening sentence and read it from the perspective of the oak trees themselves, another interpretation shows itself.

Read literally, the scripture says that before God appeared to Abraham disguised as the three visitors, God appeared to Abraham in the oak trees. We might remember here the sacred name YHWH. Although often translated LORD, this is an ultimately unpronounceable name with no vowels that can only be pronounced, or approximately pronounced, by breathing. We might translate it as Wind/Breath/Spirit of the World/Life. Genesis 18:1 says that Abraham sees this sacred Wind/Breath/Spirit in the oak trees. We can think about the way leaves rustle and quiver in the wind. We can think about how even a gentle breeze can inhabit and wear a tree like we wear clothing, making the tree appear fuller, more alive, a bit puffed up. We can think about how trees are always breathing out what we breathe in and breathing in what we breathe out in that sacred exchange of wind and breath and spirit that makes life possible. We look at the wind in a tree and we see: this is the rhythm of life on our planet. This is God's wisdom made visible. When we open our eyes to the rush of wind in a tree, we open our eyes to God. And this is where Abraham sees God first. It is only when Abraham opens his eyes to the presence of God breathing in the oak trees that he is able to see that same presence of God breathing in the human beings that visit him, thirsty for a glass of water and hungry for a bite to eat.

The oak trees teach hospitality then, both as a way of life marked by extravagant generosity and abundance, and also as a way of seeing— seeing the divine presence, the breath of life, coursing, connecting, commingling in all things, people, trees, caterpillars.

✳ ✳ ✳

It's early October, the season of painted leaves, and I've been wandering the woods in northern Wisconsin for the last half hour. White oaks dominate the forest I am in, rising tall and straight until they branch out into a canopy of copper, tan, dusty yellow leaves and taupe, jaunty squirrels. There is a party of colors above my head and an afterparty below my feet. It is perhaps the most dramatically beautiful thing that happens on the landscape here each year, as summer's sea of green slowly at first and then in rapid succession morphs and blends and fades and explodes into a fully stocked crayon box of color. Chrome yellow ash, lemon yellow aspen, and yellow orange birch fill out part of the color wheel. The maples take care of all the possible shades of red. The oaks can seem to paint with all the colors at once. Overhead, each tree comes to the party donning its particular candidate for color of the year. Underfoot the leaves mingle in a confetti carpet that makes the foot traveler feel like a high fashion celebrity walking the red carpet.

That all of this beauty is a result of the death of the trees' leaves is deeply stirring. On a crisp, lightly breezy day like today, the leaves overhead and underfoot chime back and forth to one another—a taut, crisp, confident, cheerful sound. There is no fear of death in their last words, in this leafy postlude on the turning of the year. When an oak leaf lets go of its branch, its friendly hand waves goodbye to its siblings above before flipping over and offering a friendly hello to its companions waiting below. It settles on the party-colored forest floor for a time of interspecies commingling before its season of deeper union comes when all the spent leaves come together in creating the humus below. This humus will feed the trees in seasons to come, and the leaves will find themselves rising up to the top of the canopy once more. Thoreau, in "Autumnal Tints," the final essay of his life, rightly called the fall leaves "the flower," "the harvest," and "the ripe fruit" of the year. They speak to us of the endless mystery of death and resurrection. In their radical hospitality, they stoop and fall in order to rise again.

"How beautifully they go to their graves," Thoreau wrote. "They that soared so loftily, how contentedly they return to dust again, and are laid low, resigned to lie and decay at the foot of the tree, and afford nourishment to new generations of their kind, as well as to flutter on high! They teach us how to die."

When Sarah dies before he does, Abraham purchases a plot of land "near Mamre." He purchases "both the field and the cave in it, and all the trees within the border of the field" (Genesis 23:17). He mourns and weeps over his wife and then buries her in the cave. Later when Abraham breathed his last and died "in a good old age," as scripture puts it, he was buried in the same cave, which scripture describes as "east of Mamre."

On one end of the field, I picture the cave and on the other, to the west, the oaks Abraham and Sarah so loved to camp beneath and learn from during their long and abundant and influential lives. I imagine Abraham chose this particular spot because he wanted one last view of the sun setting behind the oaks of Mamre, those masters of hospitality at whose feet he studied. I picture the low light highlighting the dark solid trunk and the bouquet of branches etched against the glowing horizon. The last flickers of the sun dance in the spirit-filled leaves. Abraham wanted a view of the oaks of Mamre, because when he died, he wanted a view of God.

3

TREE MEDICINE
ELIJAH UNDER THE BROOM TREE

Silence my soul, these trees are prayers.
I asked the tree, "Tell me about God";
then it blossomed.

—Rabindranath Tagore

It was supposed to have been his moment of greatest success, cementing his status in the pantheon of Hebrew Prophets. Elijah had just defeated the prophets of Baal once and for all in an epic showdown on Mount Carmel. After being thoroughly trounced in a shamanic duel, not one of the rival prophets makes it off the mountain alive. King Ahab and the other witnesses bow down in reverence to Elijah and to the God of Israel that the prophet represents. And not only was God's preeminence on display in the contest, but immediately following, off in the distance, a much-needed rain cloud is spotted on the horizon, signaling the end of a crippling drought. Elijah appears to be a double victor, winning the contest at hand while also solving the larger problem of the land. Full of the spirit of God he runs down the mountain in a scene of rapturous glee, thinking perhaps that finally he will be given a proper coronation as the court prophet of King Ahab and Queen Jezebel.

Sometimes in life one moment you're riding high, and the very next you can feel like you've hit rock bottom. So it was for Elijah, as we turn the page on him running with joy down the mountain. In his joy, it seems, he had miscalculated Queen Jezebel's response to recent events. Rather than celebrating the prophet, Jezebel wants him killed. She sends a message to Elijah that pops his balloon of joy and hope. By this time tomorrow, she says, she swears on her own life that Elijah's life will be in her hands. Elijah stops in his tracks and spins around on his heels. Full of fear, he runs for his life. When he makes it to the edge of the wilderness, he takes leave of his servant. He walks on alone into the desert, wondering perhaps—how did I get here? Wondering—if what I've been doing has led me here, running for my life, alone in the desert, then what's the point of it all really, what's the meaning of this? At the depths of his existential crisis, he comes upon a solitary broom tree in the middle of the desert. He sits down in the shade under the tree and he tells God that he's had enough, that he's at the end of his rope, that he's no longer running for his life, but that he has had enough of life, that he's ready to die.

This is one of the many instances in which the Bible takes an unrelentingly realistic look at the human condition and fearlessly plumbs the depths of grief, suffering, and despair. I find it interesting that when Elijah asks God to take his life, God doesn't respond to Elijah in a direct way, like God just had in helping the prophet win the duel. God doesn't solve the prophet's problem in a straightforward way by sweeping away the despair. Instead, Elijah sits with these feelings for a while under the broom tree until he falls asleep. With his head resting on a pillow of leaves and his legs stretching out on a bed of tree roots, the prophet turns his despair over to the dark dream world and offers up his sighs to the low broom branches between him and the starry night sky.

Sometime in the night, an angel from God visits the prophet. Shaking the prophet awake, the angel tells the prophet to get up and eat. And behold, there is a hot cake baking on some coals and a pitcher of water. The prophet eats, drinks, and promptly falls asleep again. The angel returns a second time. Again, the angel shakes the prophet awake and offers round two of nourishment, a second break-fast. Not only does the angel offer physical nourishment this time, but a sort of spiritual encouragement as well. You need this food and water, the angel says, because you've got a long journey ahead of you. In other words, God isn't done with you yet. I imagine this as a life-saving moment for the prophet, a moment in which his sense of pur-pose or vocation is restored, a moment when life takes on the color of meaning again. One of the ancient legends about this scripture says that when the angel visited the prophet the second time, the broom tree burst into bloom.

* * *

There's an uncanny way in which trees seem to provide exactly what we need. From oxygen for breathing to fruits and nuts for eating to sap for drinking and sweetening to wood for building and heating and shade for cooling, trees meet us and provide for us in our most basic creaturely needs. They also seem to be able to provide for us in our times of greatest acute need. Although medicines from trees (like aspirin from willow bark) have long been known, recently the more general healing power of trees is being revealed. Studies show that those recovering in a hospital after surgery recover quicker and with less depression if they have a view of trees from their room. Follow-ing these studies, New York's Mount Sinai Hospital, for example, has been redesigned so that all the recovery wards have a view of the trees in Central Park.

TREES

V, formerly Eve Ensler, playwright and author of *The Vagina Monologues* among other works, recounts her own healing encounter with a tree in *In the Body of the World: A Memoir of Cancer and Connection*. At 59, V was in the Democratic Republic of the Congo, working to help victims of rape and torture create a sanctuary called City of Joy when she received the diagnosis that she had stage 3–4 uterine cancer. Herself a victim of physical and sexual abuse at an early age, V often uses the word "embodiment" to describe her life's work—fully inhabiting our bodies and the body of this world. Trauma, she notes, has the tendency to disembody us. V tells of her lifelong struggle to fully inhabit her body and connects it to a struggle to embrace the earth and organic lifeforms like trees. She tells about a vivid memory when at twenty-two, she graduated from Middlebury College at the base of Vermont's Green Mountains and sped as quickly as she could down the highway to New York City. "Fucking trees," she remembers saying to herself. "I never want to see another tree." She looks back on this now as a time of being broken, cynical, disembodied, and despairing.

It came as a great surprise to her that it was a tree that ended up being a major source of healing and hope as she recovered from cancer and chemotherapy forty years later. "What I hadn't anticipated (in the recovery process)," she writes, "was the tree. I was too weak to think or write or call or even watch a movie. All I could do was stare at the tree, which was the only thing in my view. At first it annoyed me and I thought I would go mad from boredom. But after the first days and many hours, I began to see the tree. On Tuesday I meditated on bark; on Friday, the green leaves shimmering in late afternoon light. For hours I lost myself, my body, my being dissolving into tree."

Among other things, the tree helped her heal from a certain American impulse towards endless production and productivity, a capitalist worldview that impatiently churns towards a future of more without pause to rest in the moment and appreciate what is, simply for being what it is. "Without work or effort," she reflects on her internalized, capitalist worldview, "without providing my worth, I had no right or reason to be here. Life itself was inconsequential unless it led to something. Unless the tree would be wood, would be house, would be table, what value was there to tree? So to actually lie in my hospital bed and see tree, enter the tree, to find the green life inherent in tree, this was the awakening."

After a lifetime of animosity towards trees, it was a tree that helped spur her healing and indeed her salvation—as she describes feeling saved back into her body and back into the body of the world. She says that she still doesn't know what kind of tree it was. But on the day before she was discharged from the hospital, the tree burst into beautiful white blossoms, leaving V giddy with "insane delight."

The cancer, however, continued to besiege her body. She once again found herself back in that hospital, "back in the room with the tree." She describes coming back to the hospital feeling lonely and deeply sad. "Some part of me," she writes, "didn't want to cooperate or move forward." In tears and in pain, she describes passing out, losing consciousness for some time.

"When I woke up," she writes, "my bag was full and life, it seemed, was coursing through me. The tree had worked its magic. What I didn't know was that the tree was actually inside me and saving my life. It turns out that Taxol, one of my chemo chemicals, is found in the bark of the ancient yew tree. Even better, the Taxol is made from the needles of the tree, so the tree does not have to be destroyed. Taxol functions to stabilize the cell structure so solidly that killer cells cannot divide and multiply. It was a tree that was calming and protecting me, fortifying my cell structure so it was safe from attack."

"I had finally found," she concludes, "my mother."

※ ※ ※

In the early 1980s, Japanese government officials started to notice adverse health effects on their rapidly urbanizing, tech boom population.

They noticed increasing trends towards depression, anxiety, distraction, and bodily aches and pains. To address this public health concern, in 1982 the government introduced to the public the concept of *shinrin yoku* (森林浴), which translates as "forest bathing." They encouraged citizens to head to the forests regularly to take in the calming—and perhaps healing—power of trees. Based on Shinto and Buddhist practices, *shinrin yoku* involves bathing in the forest atmosphere by way of letting the natural landscape of trees into your body through the five senses. The sound of the forest, the scent of the trees (trees release pleasing and calming essential oils, called phytoncides), the play of sunlight on leaf canopy, the sharply clean air. Such a forest bath can quickly restore mood, restore energy, refresh us, and rejuvenate us. Indeed, research on the therapeutic benefits of forest bathing have linked time spent among trees to lower blood pressure, lower stress hormones, immune system boost, improved sleep and creativity, and help in treating depression. Japan now has sixty-two designated "forest bathing" woods which attract five million visitors annually. The practice seems to be catching on and growing around the world. South Korea, for example, has developed an ambitious National Forest Plan aimed at increasing opportunities for *shinrin yoku*, with thirty-four designated healing forests where they offer prenatal classes in the woods, forest kindergartens, addiction treatment gardens, forest burial options, and forest yoga for those suffering from PTSD, among other healing programs. We are just beginning to wake up, it seems, to the healing power of trees.

Also arising out of the Shinto and Zen Buddhist traditions of Japan, we find another tree-honoring tradition known as *hanami* (花見), literally "flower viewing" or "watching blossoms." The practice refers to the tradition of gathering in small parties beneath the trees as they bloom in spring, especially the *sakura*, or cherry tree. The roots of *hanami* stretch back to at least the year 700 CE, where we find accounts of farmers climbing up the mountain foothills to worship under the cherry trees, sensing that the blossoms held something of the spirit of spring, the spirit of fertility, new life, and growth, and so the farmers would sit under the flowering *sakura* and pray for a good planting season.

These days *hanami* is often marked by small gatherings of friends and family meeting under the flowering trees for a type of potluck gathering, eating, drinking, playing music, reciting poetry. And of course, meditating and praying—as these delicate petals are one of nature's great calls to attention—a call to awareness in the present moment, a call to be mindful of the fragile, beautiful, transient, and fleeting nature of life.

For the short window of a week or two in mid-May, I've been trying my hand at cultivating a *hanami* practice with a mature flowering crabapple that I've been blessed to live next to in this Lemon Fair valley we both call home. Each year, as the buds grow a deeper and deeper red-magenta color, the anticipation builds—will today be the day, or maybe tomorrow? And then when it happens, when the white petals burst open, it's like fireworks for the next week or two, before the wind and the rain, before the passage of time and the turning of the seasons, sends the blossoms scattered to the ground, a confetti-toss of white petals on green grass.

> What a strange thing!
> to be alive
> beneath cherry blossoms.

> A world of grief and pain,
> but the flowers bloom
> even then.
>
> —Kobayashi Issa

Hanami is a chance to celebrate the blossoming as a season that is powerful, glorious, and intoxicating, while also emotionally poignant for being so brief and short lived. The blossoms are a visual reminder that our lives, too, are both glorious and brief. *Hanami* greets us with an existential challenge and question—why not marvel at our own fleeting time on earth with the same joy and passion as we marvel at the blossoming flowers? Now is the time, the blossoms remind us, to wake up and fully embrace—fully inhabit—our impermanent bodies and the impermanent, briefly gorgeous body of the earth.

❋ ❋ ❋

The broom tree, *Retama raetam*, also known as the white broom and the white weeping broom tree, is a short, dense desert tree indigenous to the Middle East and North Africa. Although called a tree, to many it might appear more like a large shrub or bush with a broad canopy. From January to April, the broom tree is one of the most beautiful sights in the desert, as it adorns itself in a profusion of white flowers emitting a fragrant, sweet honey scent. As one of the first desert plants to bloom in the winter, the broom tree is a symbol of renewal. Its seeds speak of renewal as well with their thick coating that allows them to lie dormant for years. The seeds can survive fires and indeed mass germinations occur only after fire destroys the seed coats.

Desert travelers would have immediately understood the reference to Elijah waking up to a warm cake baking on coals. The broom tree is prized for its wood which produces the hottest and longest lasting fires in that area. The Bedouins would trade broom tree coals as a type of currency. Wandering shepherds were known to form a small mattress-sized layer of broom embers on the ground and cover them with two to four inches of sand. These sand-covered embers would keep them warm during the cold desert night.

Perhaps Elijah had such a radiant mattress as he slept under the broom tree. Providing cooling shade by day and warm embers to sleep and cook with by night, providing the wake-up call of brief and glorious beauty in its sudden burst of blossoms, under the broom tree Elijah finds hope in a hopeless place, and he's given his life back to him, his sense that God isn't done with him yet, his purpose and passion, his calling, and his joy.

4

EVERY TREE A TREE OF LIFE

Even if I knew that tomorrow the world would go to pieces,
today I would still plant my apple tree.

—Martin Luther

It's the first Sunday of Advent and we're out in the woods as a young family. We've wrapped our three-week-old daughter in as much wool and sheepskin as we could, and yet her nose and cheeks still glow peach in the crisp air. With a few inches of new snow on the ground, we delight in reading to her the story of last night's adventures in rabbit and bobcat tracks. Three weeks into new parenthood, we're a combination of exhausted, exasperated, and totally blissed out. What everyone said in advance is true: your lives will be changed forever. And yet, in some sense, the opposite is also true. Starting a new family is an invitation to reflect back on family history and to choose certain traditions to return to and repeat. One part change and one part continuity, as the story of life begins its next chapter. A new bud or branch sprouts from the Tree of Life.

We are in the woods today returning to a beloved family tradition of my youth—foraging for our own wild Christmas tree. In many publicly owned forests, permits are available at a minimal fee. This year we've paid two dollars. When I was a child, my dad would take me and my two siblings, along with a sled and an axe, into this same county forest to find our Christmas tree. It was a wonderfully exciting adventure, as if we were going hunting, which in a sense we were. The warm, heady smell of pine against the cold, cleansing smell of snow sharpened the excitement. As a family of ultra-competitive siblings, part of the thrill was the competition that we knew was soon to come. Who would get to pick this year's tree, and more importantly, who would be the one to strike the final axe blow and fell the tree? We each got five whacks before we had to pass the axe over to the next person. The progress was always slow at first, and then fast and sudden at the end as the tree trunk snapped and the small balsam fir or jack pine or spruce fell in a cloud puff of snow and ice crystals.

My dad would usually prevail in picking out the tree, and it seemed that he would always pick the scrawniest one he could find. The Charlie Brown Christmas tree was his ideal. Or maybe he was simply thinking about the long-term health of the forest in a way that we young ones weren't quite yet, leaving the healthier trees to flourish. "A conservationist," as Aldo Leopold put it in *A Sand County Almanac*, "is one who is humbly aware that with each stroke of the axe he is writing his signature on the face of the land." I look back and see our early excursions with axe in hand into the wooded winter wonderland as an early education in conservationism and ecological stewardship. I share this little bit of wisdom with my infant daughter, about Aldo Leopold and my father's Charlie Brown trees, knowing that I'll likely repeat this bit again and again over the years to come. One part change, one part continuity, and the story of life goes on.

Once felled, we would strap the tree to the wooden toboggan that we would only ever seem to use for this purpose, and we would take turns dragging the tree back to the car. Bringing the tree inside the house was the next moment of excitement, as the fragrant pine would quickly turn the whole house into a forest. Once in its stand, water was poured on the wounded trunk in hopes of keeping this evergreen symbol of eternal life vibrant for as long as possible. And then the decoration party would begin. My mom would prepare garlands of popcorn and cranberries for the tree. I didn't understand this at the time, but the tradition of putting fruit on the tree harkens back to the medieval origins of the Christmas tree tradition in northern Europe. Starting around 1500 CE, pine trees were brought into family homes to honor the Name Day of Adam and Eve (December 24). Families would decorate their trees with fruit—apples were a popular choice—in honor of these two founding humans. Paradise Trees, they were called.

Along with the popcorn and cranberries, we would decorate the boughs with all sorts of ornaments and trinkets—birds and woodland creatures, snowshoes and skis, planet-like shiny balls, star-like lights, a lone robot ornament that was my personal favorite. And then near the top, near the appropriately called crown of the tree, a circle of angels. And at the very top of the crown, the largest ornament of them all, the star of heaven. Gifts at the base of the tree would show up a few days later, completing the festive diorama.

Recalling it all now, it suddenly strikes me that the Christmas tree tradition is but a localized version of the global Tree of Life motif. A Tree of Life—sometimes called the World Tree, Cosmic Tree, Sacred Tree, Axis Mundi, Ladder to Heaven—is one of if not the most universal of all human mythical and symbolic archetypes. To name but a few, in Hinduism it is known as Ashvattha; in the Norse *Poetic Edda*, it is Yggdrasil; to the Mayans it is Yaxche. With roots that stretch to the underground, with a trunk and branches firmly planted in this world, and with a crown that reaches towards the sky, the Tree of Life participates in the three basic realms of existence. Outliving us by hundreds of years, the tree speaks to our longing for eternal life. Outgrowing us by hundreds of feet, the tree speaks to our desire for heaven. Whether staying green year-round or cycling through the seasons of birth, growth, death, and rebirth, the tree embodies the eternal lifegiving force and generative death and resurrection energy of the cosmos itself. And here we are bringing a tree like this into our homes. On its branches we decorate it with the ten thousand things of this world—foxes, pheasants, cranberries, angels, robots. At its top we place symbols of transcendence and the realm of heaven. At its base where the roots might be, a pile of gifts reminds us that life comes to us as sheer grace. The unearned, extravagant gratuity of the cosmos, wrapped in paper and tied up with a tinsel bow. What is the Christmas tree, then, but a family-sized Tree of Life? The World Tree, miniaturized to fit within the domestic world of the human home.

Of the many unearned gifts that I've opened beneath the Christmas tree, the ones I remember best are the homemade ones. Not every year, but every few years, a special gift from my grandma would appear under the tree. About the size of a book report, she would present us with copies of the latest findings from her genealogical research as she traced the history of our family. I now see those Christmas family gatherings as robust Tree of Life celebrations. As the history and stories of the family are passed down, the branches of the tree fill in and grow.

As we find our tree for this year—a scrawny balsam fir growing too close for comfort to a robust white oak with hopefully still another few hundred years to go—I pause to give thanks to the forest from which this tree comes. I pause to ask permission to harvest the gift of this one tree. I tell the forest about Christmas as a Tree of Life holiday. I pray for the health of the land as I remember how to hold the axe, as I plan my first five strikes. I look forward to bringing this World Tree into the new nest that we're creating as a young family, as soon we'll add our own ornaments and gifts will appear and a star will be placed on its wobbly crown. We'll gather this year with a new bud on our family tree. In some sense, our lives are forever changed. In another, we're returning to and repeating what has been. One part change, one part continuity, and the Tree of Life lives on.

* * *

The last chapters of Revelation which culminate in the final Tree of Life image present the most detailed and striking vision of what Jesus often talked about as the kingdom of God—that dream of a more beautiful world yet-to-come, a world of redemption, shalom, salvation; a world where God will dwell with us and, as the scripture imagines it, "death will be no more, and mourning and crying and pain will be no more," and we will see things in the true light of God, even seeing God, no longer "through a glass darkly" as we do in this life, but with perfect clarity, face-to-face. And right in the middle of this redeemed world our scripture imagines that there will be a Tree of Life, "with its twelve kinds of fruit, producing its fruit each month; and the leaves of the tree are for the healing of the nations."

The way many people talk about it, heaven is a place beyond this world where people go when they die, often imagined directionally as up, as in "we go up to heaven when we die." According to the vision in Revelation, in the end people don't go up to heaven, but heaven, the holy realm, comes down to us. God comes down to earth to dwell with us, and the Tree of Life is planted here, not in some other world beyond this one, but on this very earth, in this very world.

This is a thoroughly ecological vision that imagines this earth as the location of salvation. It's one thing to think that God is preparing an unimaginably beautiful heaven-palace for us in a world beyond this one, something like whatever we might dream is beyond the pearly gates. But it's an entirely different way of thinking about it to look around at this world—even with its injustices, and heartbreak, and unmet longing— and to see it as a world getting ready for heaven to arrive. To look around and to think about preparing this world as a place that's fit for God to dwell. Revelation and the Tree of Life invite us not to try to see or envision a different world, but to see and envision this world differently.

Today, our relationship to the earth's climate is the most pressing manner in which we've been taking a fateful step in the wrong direction, away from the kingdom of God. And perhaps unsurprisingly, our relationship to trees is at the heart of it, as for the last few hundred years we have been rapidly releasing the energy that trees had patiently stored up for thousands of years and sequestered underground. What we've been burning to power our global civilization are dead trees. The amount of tree energy that we've unleashed into the earth's system is almost unfathomable. Recent oceanic heating studies suggest we've been releasing the equivalent of one atomic bomb per second for the last 150 years. Today the effect is something on the magnitude of three to six Hiroshima nuclear bombs being detonated in the ocean every single second.[58a]

At the same time that we've been burning long dead trees and unleashing their carbon, we've also been cutting down living trees. According to a study by Yale University, there are currently about three trillion living trees on earth. That number, however, is declining by about fifteen billion trees per year. It is thought that there are almost fifty percent fewer trees on earth today than there were before humans started cutting them down. A mature tree absorbs carbon dioxide from the atmosphere at a rate of forty-eight pounds per year, and releases oxygen in exchange. An acre of forest is able to sequester about the CO_2 usage equivalent of two American households. We have never invented a machine as efficient at turning CO_2 into O_2. And even if we did, can you imagine what such a machine would look like? It's unlikely to come anywhere close to the beauty of a tree. Of course, if just planting more trees were all that we did for the climate, we would fall far short of the radical lifestyle and economic changes that the earth is calling out for at this moment. But planting trees is certainly part of it. And perhaps a larger part of it than we might imagine.

Every Tree a Tree of Life

Our relationship to trees, the Bible seems to intuit, is indicative of our relationship to the earth as a whole. Trees are metonyms for our stewardship of the entire creation. How we relate to trees reveals how we relate to others, to the earth, to God. And trees can be like our window and invitation back into interdependence and interconnection. Because at the end, the Tree of Life is awaiting us—that ultimate symbol of the indivisible, integral, interconnected web of life.

✳ ✳ ✳

After about as much anticipation as a six-week-old can muster, Christmas morning has finally arrived. We gather with coffee and blueberry muffins and try to make sense of the heap of gifts that rests under the tree. Where did they all come from, we wonder, when really it's the abundance of life itself—where did all this cosmos come from?—that fills wonder with wonder. I notice there are at least two gifts that appear to be the ideal size of one of my grandma's book reports from her family tree research. And indeed, one of them is the latest chapter about her grandfather. Paul Eriksen, we read, was born out of wedlock to sixteen-year-old Ane. She did the best she could on her own to raise him, my grandma reports, having recently found his trail through a baptismal record at a small Lutheran church in rural Denmark. Without land or family support, life would have been hard for Paul in nineteenth-century Denmark, and so at seventeen he immigrated by himself to the United States. He worked hard on farms in the Upper Midwest, marrying and raising a family, before the Great Depression saw them lose their land and relocate to Chicago, where my grandma grew up. One more branch of the family tree filled in.

The other gift of that size is from my parents, a new children's book for us to read to our daughter. *Wangari Maathai: The Woman Who Planted Millions of Trees,* by author Franck Prévot and illustrator Aurélia Fronty, tells the remarkable story of the life of Wangari Maathai (1940–2011). Born near a fig tree that she was taught from an early age was holy and a Tree of Life in the central highlands of Kenya, Wangari left

137

home to study biology in the United States. When she returned to Kenya as a young adult, she was shocked at how quickly the ecosystem was being degraded, particularly how quickly deforestation was accelerating and changing not only the wellbeing of the landscape, but the wellbeing of the people. Inspired by the Civil Rights movement in the United States, Wangari decided to organize and mobilize for change. Focusing her work on trees, she started the Green Belt Movement, which incentivized 900,000 Kenyan women to take tree planting, and the future of their landscape and community, into their own hands. In Kenya, over thirty million trees have been planted as part of this movement. Worldwide the number is in the billions. Maathai came to be known affectionately as Mama Miti, "the mother of trees." In 2004, she became the first African woman to be awarded the Nobel Peace Prize. The Committee described her accomplishment as showing the world a new form of civic agency that involved standing up for nature and for humanity as an indivisible whole. "Environmental work is peace work," as she put it. "The tree became a symbol for our democratic struggle in Kenya." Planting trees was her powerful way of preparing the city of God, because "a tree is a little bit of the future," as Prévot puts it in this gorgeously illustrated and inspiring children's book about the life of our new Christmas hero this year, Mama Miti.

In the Biblical imagination, the Tree of Life is not just a little bit of the future. It is the future. Standing in for the whole evolutionary unfolding of life, for the whole generative cosmos itself, finding the Tree of Life flourishing at the end of time teaches us that our own future is inseparable from the larger, ecological community on which we are directly dependent. Looking back at us from the future—looming over us as we journey in the meantime—the Tree of Life guides us with the central tenet that graciously and fatefully and finally, all life on Earth is interconnected. The Tree of Life says right here, on this planet—this is to be the place of salvation.

Every tree is a tree of life.

CLOUDS

CREATION ELEMENT INTERLUDE: AIR

All praise be Yours, my God, through Brothers Wind and Air,
And fair and stormy, all the weather's moods,
By which You cherish all that You have made.

—ST. FRANCIS OF ASSISI, *CANTICLE OF THE SUN*

If the universe begins with fire, if biotic life begins with water, if creaturely life begins with earth, then we might say that the individual spirit or soul, or the inward mind and consciousness of life, begins with the air element. Genesis 2 imagines this beautifully in that moment when God breathes into the inanimate clay figure the animating breath of life. Genesis 1 prefigures that moment when the human spirit was first breathed into being by imagining the *ruach* of God—the Spirit/Breath/Wind of God—hovering over the primordial waters, signaling that a creative consciousness was beginning to stir. As with the Hebrew *ruach*, the Greek *pneuma* also means both spirit and wind/air/breath. The air element is the life inside of life, and literally so, as life exists only through the constant cadence of inhale, exhale. Our lives begin with a piercing birth cry as we gasp for our first breath, and our lives end when we stop breathing, as our last sigh dissipates and merges back into the universal reservoir of air. Our personalities, our minds, our souls come from the nothingness of air and when we die they return from whence they came.

If the air element speaks to the unique spirit or soul within all living things, it also speaks to life's radical enmeshment. As we all breathe in and breathe out, air connects us with all of life, both currently as well as with all the life that has preceded us, and all the life that will come after us on this planet. Teilhard de Chardin called it "the breathing together of all things." We absorb something of the spirit and atmosphere of the planet and the life that it hosts, graciously and fatefully connected through a vast interflow of the air element, making God and the sacredness of life as close to us as the air we breathe.

Spiritual traditions across the world have understood this primordial air intimacy by making attention to breath foundational for meditative and contemplative practices. Noticing our breath brings us into the present moment. If the earth element harbors ancient memory in its geological layering, and if water and fire rush and burn ahead towards the future, then air is an in-the-moment, present thing. We breathe in and we breathe out and we are in the moment because the air element is a present moment element. Air is now.

In the New Testament, the Holy Spirit is an exquisite metaphor for the sacredness of the air element. It is imagined as a rush of wind at Pentecost and as an aerial dove descending from the sky at Jesus's baptism. In John's Gospel, the resurrected Christ leaves the disciples with the final gift of the Holy Spirit by breathing on them (John 20:22). In one of his most poetic teachings about the spirit of God, Jesus compares the way of spirit to the spontaneity of wind, stating that like wind, spirit "blows where it wishes." I think about how a tree can be full of wind in one moment, leaning hard to the side, and then after the wave of wind crashes and settles, the tree goes quiet and listless.

As Celtic philosopher and poet John O'Donohue describes in *The Four Elements: Reflections on Nature*, air, as the only invisible element, is close to the unknown and the unknown is close to the spontaneous and the surprising. Air is an uncanny element. We are surrounded by it, always dependent on it, and yet we cannot see it. Like the deepest of truths—beauty, goodness, justice, peace, music, God, grace—we can sense air, but we cannot see it. We see it only in its aftereffect—swaying grass, rustling leaves, rippling water, wisping clouds.

Often in mythological and religious traditions, the air element goes by the beautiful name of sky. The sky is the counterpoint to the earth and is often imagined as a masculine element to earth's feminine generativity—Father Sky and Mother Earth. The sky is a natural symbol for heaven and transcendence, as when we look out at the sky, we see no end. We sense infinity and we hope in the possibility of a realm beyond all beyonds.

For the scope of this project, I have decided to focus on the main feature that gives a sense of dimension and personality to the sky: the clouds. I think of the clouds as the artists of the air element, or the art that the air element makes when it picks up its paint of water and light. Unlike us earthbound creatures, and unlike birds which also tend in the end to be earthbound, clouds are entirely at home in the air element. And as they seem midway between us and the planets, the clouds have long been sensed as the abode of the gods, and as natural phenomena through which spiritual revelation consistently manifests.

As they grace our days and our planet with shade and rain and variety, clouds make the invisible air element visible, and in so doing they make the invisibility of God visibly playful, powerful, graceful, marvelous.

I

THE HEAVENS ARE TELLING
THE GLORY OF GOD

All other creatures look down toward the earth,
but humanity was given a face so that they might turn their eyes
toward the stars and their gaze upon the sky.

—OVID, *METAMORPHOSES*

Today I look out on rows of high, whiteout cirrus unfurling against a cobalt blue stained-glass troposphere. Cirrus uncinus as they're known, from the Latin for "lock" or "curl" of hair, and "hooked." Folklore names them mares' tails, and indeed, when grouped or layered together like they are today, they seem like a herd galloping into the wind, charging off into an open field of sky. Upon closer attention, they have a distinct painterly or brushwork quality, as if done by an artist with a confident if quick, playful, romantic, and abstract line. Upon closer attention still, the painting is churning, changing, alive in a way no painting in a museum could ever be.

CLOUDS

And much like with a visit to a great museum, taking a moment to take in the clouds leaves me with the feeling that the drab dust of the everyday has been washed off, and the world is polished and transparent again to beauty and possibility. Ralph Waldo Emerson put it well when he described the clouds and the sky as "the daily bread of the eyes, the ultimate art gallery above."

The poet of Psalm 19 saw the sky and the clouds along the same lines, as masterpieces in creation's permanent collection. "The heavens are telling the glory of God; the sky proclaims the work of God's hands," the poet writes, in verses that C.S. Lewis deemed to be "the greatest poem in the Psalter and one of the greatest lyrics in the world." The Hebrew word for "heaven" here is *shamayim*, which has the same meaning and is elsewhere translated simply as "sky."* Coming from root words *esh* (fire) and *mayim* (water), *shamayim* is a beautiful, poetic way of referring to the heavens as the combination of fire and water— the sky as the domain of sun and cloud. The Hebrew word translated as "sky" in the second half of the verse is *raqia*, meaning an expanse or an extended surface. With this first verse of Psalm 19, we have something more literally like: the beautiful skies are telling the glory of God; the expansive skies proclaim the work of God's hands.

This first verse is a paradigmatic example of the type of parallel structure that is key to understanding the Hebrew poetry of the Bible. Hebrew poetry tends to work by way of presenting two lines at a time that both aim to express nearly the same sentiment or to express the same idea but in two different ways (or with two stitches, as each half of the verse is referred to technically as a hemistich). In other words, it uses language as a type of homing device, using words to circle around an idea, even an idea as hard to talk about as God, homing in, circling

---

*Sky—c. 1200, "a cloud," from Old Norse sky "cloud," from Proto-Germanic skeujam "cloud, cloud cover" (source also of Old English sceo, Old Saxon scio "cloud, region of the clouds, sky;" Old High German scuwo, Old English scua, Old Norse skuggi "shadow;" Gothic skuggwa "mirror"), from PIE root (s)keu- "to cover, conceal." (source: etymonline.com)

around, the way a moth circles around a flame. Psalm 19:1 is, in my estimation, about as close to being seared by the flame of God as any words can come.

Psalm 19 can be read as a daytime companion piece to Psalm 8's midnight meditation on the stars. In both poems, the wonder of what is displayed by the stars and moon at night and by the clouds and sun by day transports or elevates the human heart into communion with God. In both poems, the celestial phenomena of stars and clouds are instances in which we can witness the hand of God at work in creation. They are occasions to trace the fingerprints of God, as these poems make direct reference to God's hands (Psalm 19) and God's fingers (Psalm 8). The feeling is one of dizzying, dazzling intricacy and immensity—that the things of heaven, the stars and the clouds, as distant and vast as they are, are but miniature figurines, the playthings of God's fingertips.

The herd of mares' tails above me today keep running and racing towards the horizon. Looking at them with Psalm 19 in mind, I can almost see God's hands at play in what must be the most virtuosic finger painting the world has ever seen. It's the most contemporary art there is, made for just this moment in just this place, like a poem written in chalk on a sidewalk just before a rainstorm. Later and elsewhere, new shows go on and on. It is the ultimate art gallery, always and everywhere open and free to the public, if only we but lift our eyes.

❊ ❊ ❊

The best commentary that I know on Psalm 19:1 is not by a theologian but by a journalist. In a *Boston Globe* article titled "Looking at the Sky Might Change Your Entire POV," journalist Jan Brogan details her journey towards cloud and sky awareness. Her journey was prompted by a cryptic email she received one day. "Look at the sky as often as you 'can'—for about 21 days. I'll contact you again in 3 wks." Signed, "More Light."

CLOUDS

This challenge was issued to her by Jack Borden, a former Boston television reporter who started For Spacious Skies, a nonprofit organization advocating the cause of "sky awareness." This is a cause that I had never heard of or even imagined existing before this article, but that seems surprisingly appropriate in this age of quickening climate chaos, in which clouds are the most literal "writing in the sky" for us to pay attention to and heed. Lamenting our general lack of attention paid to the sky and to the clouds, Borden is quoted as saying, "When we are unconscious in regard to our surroundings, we are irresponsible to them."

For Jan, the three-week challenge to look at the sky began without much fanfare. Day 1: Jan writes, "'Some clouds and a lot of blue sky.' I go back to work at the computer."

After a few days, though, she begins to notice more about the details of the sky, even beginning to identify certain clouds by type: cumulus and altocumulus; stratus and cirrus. She begins to make connections between cloud formations and precipitation patterns, even predicting tomorrow's forecast based on today's sky.

It's not long before paying attention to the sky yields something like spiritual dividends, as when, on Day 10, looking to the sky helps smooth her traffic-laden commute: "Stop-and-go traffic just before 4 o'clock, heading west on Route 109. I divert myself by looking at the different shades of sky: deep blue, periwinkle, and aqua. Ahead, the clouds are tattered, low on the horizon, and under-lit by the sun. I do not try to identify the clouds by type, which I think might wreck the moment."

By Day 21, she finds herself a changed person. After she identifies the clouds overhead as the type of high cirrus that tend to usher in a cold front, she notes the transition in her experience from the observational to the spiritual dimensions of this sky watching practice. "I like having this type of knowledge [of the cloud types]," she writes, "but there is something else going on. It seems amazingly self-centered to have so narrowly focused my visual field until now that I did not bother to notice the medium I lived in. The draw is not so much the beauty of the sky every day, but the enormity of it."

She concludes her field notes on sky awareness with this exchange she has with her teenage daughter: "My daughter walks into the office, sees the sky chart, asks if I am still into that 'sky thing' or if I am bored yet. I hear myself tell her that I don't think I could ever be bored by the sky."

※　※　※

At the Ringling Museum of Art in Sarasota, Florida there is a work of art that, over my years of visiting it, has done for me what the sky awareness challenge did for Jan Brogan. That is, this work of art has encouraged me to see sky and clouds with something of the radical amazement of Psalm 19:1. To try to consider each cloud as a tap on the shoulder, a call to attention, a reminder that at every moment and everywhere, no matter what else is happening in the world or in my life, it's always the case that the heavens are telling the glory of God, and the skies proclaim the work of God's hands.

Joseph's Coat (2011) is a "Skyspace" by light artist James Turrell. The Skyspace at the Ringling is one of about a dozen Skyspaces that Turrell has created. A Turrell Skyspace, as the artist defines it, "is a specifically proportioned chamber with an aperture in the ceiling open to the sky." At the Ringling Museum, *Joseph's Coat* is housed in the Searing Wing in the middle of the museum campus. It is a building within a building, or an architectural space within the architecture of the building itself. There is one showing of the artwork per day, beginning during the golden hour and lasting until just after sunset when night falls, or as Turrell prefers to put it, when night rises. After procuring your tickets for the evening's show, you walk through the museum grounds, a winding path through stately palm trees, lily pad ponds stalked at the edges by herons and egrets, twisted live oaks with Spanish moss over fields of soft fern and scratchy St. Augustine grass.

CLOUDS

For tonight's showing, our small congregation lines up outside the Searing Wing. There is an eclectic couple with their young adult child named Raven. There is a stylish millennial couple on a date and an older couple who seem like they've been here before. And there are two parents chaperoning six elementary aged children. Driving over the Longboat Key Pass and through St. Armand's Circle, there was barely a cloud in the sky. The Skyspace is a beautiful and powerful work of art with or without clouds, but like with a classic Gulf Coast sunset, I'm of the opinion that clouds add to the beauty and the glory of it. Tellingly, after one of the cloudless showings that I recently attended, a first-timer asked me afterwards, "is it better with clouds?"

Tonight, just as I pulled into the Ringling parking lot, the sky suddenly darkened as a bank of altocumulus rose up between the museum and the late afternoon sun. I would later identify these as altocumulus stratiformis translucidus—that is, these were mid-level patches of clouds, or cloudlets, spread over a large area, and most were thin enough to still see the sun through. There was one other striking cloud type as well, as on the opposite horizon a small group of altocumulus castellanus, also known as jellyfish clouds, hung over the live oaks with delicate tentacles dangling vertically below their bell-shaped heads.

A fifteen-foot sculpture of a winged goddess, *La Gloria* by Jorge Marin, stands cast in bronze and earthbound with her face tilted in longing towards the sky, guarding the entrance as you walk up the stairs and through the first doors. After handing the docent your ticket, you walk through a second set of doors to enter the space. Tonight, as I open those second doors, it strikes me for the first time how odd this is—that this is an artwork that proposes that we go inside in order to see the sky.

Inside, the space opens up into a square room that has the indoor/outdoor feel of a courtyard, while also having the protective embrace of a chapel. The walls are daisy white with creeping fig vine working its way up the sides. White columns form a colonnade and act as large trellises for star jasmine vines. Cedar benches surround a center stage of stone tiled flooring, raised a bit in the middle, with grates for rain runoff. Above, the white ceiling covers only part of the room, as there is a twenty-four-foot square opening directly overhead acting as a frame, or an aperture through which to view the sky.

Upon entering, the feeling is of walking into an empty church on a quiet weekday. That this has the feeling of a sacred space is intentional. Turrell grew up in the Quaker tradition. His first Skyspace in 1979 in New York City was titled *Meeting*, after the name for Quaker worship gatherings. In an interview, the artist said that when he made his first Skyspace, he realized he was making the Quaker meeting that he always dreamed of. He tells of how as a child he would find himself daydreaming during the silence of a meeting, and often dreamed of a '57 Ford convertible, how the metal top would retract back into the trunk, and he would imagine the same thing happening to the ceiling in the meeting room. Turrell's medium of light is a key concept in Quakerism—in the silence of a Quaker meeting, what each individual is seeking to meet is the divine light within. One goes within to greet the light. With that spiritual background in mind, perhaps the whole notion of going inside to see the sky starts to make a bit more sense.

Tonight, the sky is a warm lagoon blue and the cloudlets are basking in it, aglow in the late afternoon sun. The simple framing of the sky somehow makes the sky feel closer, as if you were looking at it through a telescope, or as if the clouds, thousands of feet above, were painted on the ceiling. The aperture suggests the feeling of being an astronaut gazing at the blue marble of planet earth through the spaceship window, except in reverse, as if the opening is a window on spaceship earth through which we look out on the distant heavens. The whole set up makes the sky the most exciting show on earth, and this is before the actual show has even begun.

You can sit on the benches or you can bring a yoga mat or towel and lie down on the floor and gaze up, or rather, out. Tonight, I've brought a sandy beach towel to lie down on and a thick wool sweater to use as a pillow. The "show" involves subtle LED lights that cast the ceiling frame in a series of colors—each hue changing by way of color theory, sometimes subtly and almost imperceptibly, sometimes dramatically and shockingly, the appearance of the sky. For the first few minutes though, there doesn't seem to be anything happening other than looking at the sky as it is. Today it is little heaps of altostratus pinned against blue sky, the frame about two-thirds sky and one-third cloud. But of course, the clouds aren't pinned down. They're moving, constantly drifting horizontally right to left like Hebrew script, speaking in the amorphous language of shapes. Against the restless clouds the sky appears like a static background, like a canvas.

Seahorse, gargoyle, turtle, phoenix shifting into dragon. Most of the clouds seem saturated with the light of the setting sun, glowing a warm, indulgent white, like crème fraiche. Some, on the other hand, seem invisible to the sun and take on the color of the blue sky, as if the same color were painted on top of itself, or as if the sky is trying to conceal itself in cloud camouflage. Now the frame is two-thirds cloud and one-third sky and an airplane glides through it like half a silver arrow, or like a flying fish hook. In its wake, the plane leaves a confident contrail line behind, as if taking a thick marker to the canvas, or as if stitching a zipper into the fabric of the sky. A small bird flits by, its sound lasting long after its appearance, like a meditation bell.

A jagged edge of cirrus arrives high above, adding a sense of depth and dimension, and bringing fire to the sky like a golden crown of sunset. The ceiling frame is now raspberry purple, making the blue clouds even bluer than the blue sky, as the cirrus fire-crown cools to yellow gold. The purple turns more pastel and the sky softens to seafoam green, the same color as the warm Gulf waters, like when a wave crests and the sun lights up the crest of the wave and the clouds in the sky-ocean above me add splashes of foam brightness like the spray coming off the waves and like the bubbles as the waves unfurl and lap up and then back down the smoothed sand edge of the beach. It strikes me that unlike the rhythmic lapping of the waves, the clouds scroll indefatigably, constantly by, and when they are gone, they do not come back again. Waves speak of a type of change that laps, that ebbs and flows, back and forth, whereas clouds tell of a change that lapses. Clouds are once and then never again.

As the ceiling turns from red to peach to yellow, the sky darkens to the deep indigo of night, although if my sense of timing is right, the sun should only just now be setting. And indeed, in another minute, the ceiling takes on a sunset apricot hue and the clouds are foregrounded again bright against the sky. The sky now seems to work and wind its way through the clouds in narrow channels like rivers winding through hills, lending a topographical quality to the sky, and it's as if I'm looking down at the sky like looking down at the earth from an airplane. The clouds are mountain ranges with height, depth, and contour. The sky is a series of rivers and lakes.

A black cormorant passes, portent of darkening night. The clouds thicken further, forming vast plateaus and highlands where no sky cuts through. Now the walls are neon blue, turning the clouds a mousy, dishwater blond. The cloud plateau beaks open, like a glacier fissuring and melting and rivers of sky run free again, although in fact it is the cloud mountains that are running and the sky water that appears static. An orange creamsicle ceiling returns the blue hue to the sky, and the sky darkens and becomes a stronger presence. The sky gathers into one major river in the middle of the frame, like the Mississippi with its own tributaries, eddies, sloughs, and islands of sky. A dark jade ceiling yields the first star sighting of the night, and in another second or two, a second and then a third pinprick through the dark sky river, marking the start of the new day according to Jewish tradition.

For a moment, a Kelly-green ceiling frames lavender cream clouds against a plum pudding sky. Green turns to blue which seems to drain the color out of the sky again, making both the clouds and the sky sepia, abstract, ancient for a moment and stuck in time like a photograph from Alfred Stieglitz's *Equivalents*. More stars and constellations of stars and suddenly it's night, although the clouds still keep some light in them, like lightbulbs that glow after being switched off.

"Good morning everyone!" the docent announces, signaling that the show is over. We leave the roofless building in wordless wonder and step out into the roofless world. Even more stars, and even more clouds, and palm tree moon shadows and the smell of jasmine and the ocean at night and the soft, slurred cooing of mourning doves. The show, of course, goes on and on. Everywhere and all the time. If only we but lift our eyes and see. The heavens are telling the glory of God. The skies are proclaiming the work of God's hands. The ultimate art gallery. Just above us. A daily feast.

2

SIGNS OF THE TIMES

Dayem semakum ghaim
(May your sky always be filled with clouds)

—TRADITIONAL IRANIAN BLESSING

It's mid-March in Wisconsin and we seem stuck in limbo, going back and forth between "False Spring" and "Third Winter." The sun has been struggling to make itself known under a blanket of stratus for the last few days, although today the blanket is beginning to come undone, the steely Great Lakes gray giving way to patches of murky whites. And ever so faint at first, like the first stars at night, patches of sky open the flat world to the blue beyond, and the sun finds a way to glow through a patch of thin clouds casting soft shadows on the thawing snow. Stratocumulus like these today are low patches and clumps of clouds with an indistinct patterning. Known in English as "twain clouds," they are a combination or they fall categorically somewhere in-between the well-formed cumulus and the formless stratus. Just taking a quick peak out the window, I might find myself judging such a day as overcast, dull, dreary. When I sit with these clouds a little longer, however, I can't help but marvel at their subtle and unpredictable variation.

That the clouds seem to have both form and formlessness makes them enigmatic in a sophisticated and artful way. They strike me as masters of ambiguity and nuance, softening the edges between dualities like light and shadow. And appearing here now near the end of winter, the random smattering of lighter patches feels, if not optimistic, then hopeful. Indeed, stratocumulus often mark either the beginning or the end of a weather front, and as this week's forecast bears out, today marks the first step into the next few days of a false spring thaw.

My initial reaction to today's clouds—overcast, dull, dreary—is indicative of a widespread negative bias against clouds, at least in the English-speaking world. When we're worried about the future, for example, we say that it feels like there's "a cloud on my horizon." Or when we're feeling down, we say we're feeling "under the weather," or that "there's a cloud hanging over me." "Every cloud has a silver lining," we say to cheer ourselves up when things are tough. The sun, we remind ourselves when we're sad, is always shining above the clouds. Just yesterday, blanketed by that steely gray stratus, I found myself singing to my infant daughter, "you are my sunshine, my only sunshine, you make me happy when skies are gray."

On the other hand, we're quick to turn to the cloudless blue sky as a metaphor for happiness. "Blue skies / smiling at me / nothing but blue skies / do I see." Or when we're feeling hopeful about the future, we talk about having a sunny outlook or a sunny disposition, or we say that there's "nothing but clear skies ahead." We strive for clear and bright ideas and deride cloudy thinking. "Blue-sky thinking" is a buzz-word in the corporate world for a type of brainstorming activity that tries to create space for the best new ideas to arise.

This tendency to associate the sun with happiness and clouds with sadness also shows up in many Christian hymns. Scanning the United

Church of Christ's *New Century Hymnal*, I'm struck by how often clouds appear as negative metaphors, as something that one would hope and pray would just go away. Here's a small sampling of some of the verses:

❊ ❊ ❊

Melt the clouds of sin and sadness,
drive the storms of doubt away

May no earth born cloud arise . . . to hide you from my eyes

Clouds of doubt dispersing

Clouds of disaster

Your chariots of wrath the deep thunderclouds form

❊ ❊ ❊

Our cultural and theological bias against clouds is particularly striking when compared with the place of clouds in the Bible, where clouds are nearly universally regarded in a positive light and praised as nothing less than the most natural and immediate signs of the presence, the promise, and the glory of God.

❊ ❊ ❊

When it looked like the sun wouldn't shine anymore
God put a rainbow in the cloud
　　　　—Nineteenth-century African-American Spiritual

The Bible's cloud-positive outlook begins with the first direct reference to clouds in the story of Noah and the Flood in Genesis 9. There we read about how after the ecological disaster of the global flood subsides, and life returns to the earth, God makes a covenant with humanity and with all creation. God pledges never to flood and threaten the future of life on earth like that again, and as a sign of that promise God points our gaze to the clouds, and particularly to that always surprising and delightful cloud phenomenon of a rainbow in the sky.

> God said, "This is the sign of the covenant that I make between me and you and every living creature that is with you, for all future generations: I have set my bow in the clouds, and it shall be a sign of the covenant between me and the earth. When I bring clouds over the earth and the bow is seen in the clouds, I will remember my covenant that is between me and you and every living creature of all flesh; and the waters shall never again become a flood to destroy all flesh. When the bow is in the clouds, I will see it and remember the everlasting covenant between God and every living creature of all flesh that is on the earth." God said to Noah, "This is the sign of the covenant that I have established between me and all flesh that is on the earth."
>
> —Genesis 9:12–17

When I bring clouds over the earth...I can imagine Noah thinking to himself—really God, more clouds? Wasn't it clouds that caused the flood in the first place? God promises to relent from all the rain, and the sign of the promise is...more clouds? It is the most unexpected and therefore the ultimate armistice. God turns the very instrument of destruction into the sign of peace. The sword into the ploughshare. The bullet into the butterfly.

The rainbow is the perfect natural phenomenon for that moment of peace and hope after the storm, as more often than not rainbows signify the end of a rain event. A rainbow is a special type of cloud phenomenon known as a cloud iridescence or irisation, named after the Greek goddess Iris, goddess of rainbows and messenger between the mortal and the immortal realms. Rainbows appear when there is enough moisture in the sky to refract sunlight, but not enough to obscure it. The water droplets break up the white light so that we see all the colors in the visible spectrum, allowing us to see that which we usually aren't able to, turning the invisible briefly visible. It is as if for a moment the sky has both rain and sunshine in it at the same time, or as if the fire element and the water element are no longer at odds, but are playmates and at peace, like the lion lying down with the lamb. In this sense, the rainbow is the perfect sign of God's covenantal promise with creation. Even more than a sign, the rainbow is a symbol of God's promise, in the sense of theologian Paul Tillich's understanding of a symbol as being a type of sign that, more than just pointing to a reality, actually and directly participates in the reality toward which it points.

Medieval Jewish interpretations keyed into this notion of armistice because the Hebrew word for rainbow carries the more general meaning of the shape of the weapon, rather than the more meteorologically specific term. Seeing the rainbow in the sky, it was as if God was pointing the bow, pointing the weapon, away from the earth. The flood was, in a sense, God pointing the bow at the earth. But the new bow—the rainbow—points away, and no longer has a string or a quiver of arrows. The rainbow is God's armistice written in the sky, God's ceasefire in the clouds. The rainbow is the Creator making peace with creation, as imperfect or as unrealized as it—as we—might be. The rainbow is God accepting and loving us unconditionally, just as we are in all our colorful diversity, which the LGBTIQIA+ community expresses so well through the rainbow pride flag.

While witnessing rainbows bring us humans so much natural and childlike delight, it's interesting to ponder that in the context of Genesis 9 the rainbow is a symbol meant not primarily for us but for God to notice and for God to be reminded of God's commitments to make peace with the earth. "When the bow is in the clouds, I will see it and remember," God says. I take from this that the rainbow, which is most often observed naturally in the form of a half circle, is also theologically a half-sign or a half-symbol. The rainbow is God's pledge not to destroy creation. In other words, God will take care of God's side of creation care. But that still leaves much for us and for the earth to do if we are to complete the circle. God guarantees that God will not destroy the world, but God cannot guarantee that the world will not destroy itself. The other side of the rainbow, the other side of the creation covenant, the other side of accepting and loving unconditionally the endlessly diverse things of nature just as they are and making a covenantal promise that we'll do absolutely whatever we can to make sure life will have a future... that half of the rainbow is up to us.

✳ ✳ ✳

At any given moment, clouds cover about two-thirds of the earth's surface, with stratocumulus alone covering one-fifth of the earth. As low clouds, stratocumulus have an overall cooling effect on the earth's climate, blocking much of the sun's energy from above. High clouds like cirrus, on the other hand, have an overall warming effect, as they act more like down comforters than beach umbrellas, capturing and keeping the earth's warmth here below. Averaging it all out, clouds in general keep the Earth's surface cooler than if there were no clouds.

The effects of our warming climate on cloud formation is quickly becoming one of the greatest unknowns and one of the greatest concerns in contemporary climate modeling. A recent study has found that if the current estimates at rising temperatures are accurate (estimates that until now have not factored clouds into their models), then the expected warming could have a dramatic impact on the future of cloud cover on the earth. And unfortunately, the warning is dire. A warming planet could lead to huge tracts of stratocumulus dissipating and burning off, especially over the oceans. If that happens, if stratocumulus cover significantly declines, this could create a warming feedback loop in which clouds would have an overall warming effect on the planet, a tipping point that would send global heating into overdrive.

Signs of the Times

✳ ✳ ✳

Humans have long looked to the clouds to try to predict the future and to plan their activities in relation to the weather forecasting that reading the clouds can yield. "Mackerel sky, mackerel sky," as sailors are known to say, "not long wet, not long dry." "Red sky at night, sailor's delight," I remember my grandpa often saying as we watched a glowing sunset while out in a small aluminum rowboat fishing on the lake. "Red sky in the morning," he would continue, "sailor's take warning." Once this ancient bit of meteorological wisdom was referenced by Jesus.

> The Pharisees and Sadducees came, and to test Jesus they asked him to show them a sign from heaven. He answered them, "When it is evening, you say, 'It will be fair weather, for the sky is red.' And in the morning, 'It will be stormy today, for the sky is red and threatening.' You know how to interpret the appearance of the sky, but you cannot interpret the signs of the times."
>
> —Matthew 16:1–3

Today we look to the clouds and we know that we need to wonder and concern ourselves not just with the weather, with what Jesus calls "the appearance of the sky," but we need to wonder and concern ourselves with what the clouds might be teaching us and warning us and urging us when it comes to the existential perils of a climate caught in warming chaos. The clouds are today's most lucid writing in the sky when it comes to climate change. They are what Jesus calls "the signs of the times."

They call to us to love and care for the future flourishing of all creation—calling out with that half of the original rainbow promise that is always and forever and urgently ours.

3

CLOUD OF WITNESSES

Wherefore seeing we also are compassed
about with so great a cloud of witnesses...

—Hebrews 12:1 (King James Version)

By noon the stratus that blanketed my world this morning has started to break up into low layers, rows, and clumps of stratocumulus. A parade of shapes and forms is playing above me, the picture changing in multiple ways at once as the shapes of the clouds themselves are changing—forming, reforming, appearing, and disappearing—while at the same time the whole frame is ceaselessly scrolling as a south wind sweeps each moment's scene away, tugging constantly as on an endless scroll of cloud. Deep fjords of searing sky blue cut through the erratically shaped, white, gray, and sandy-toned edges of the clouds. As the tidal edge of the cloud ebbs and flows, and as smaller puffs of cloud fracture and sail off on their own, shapes appear quickly, and then disappear just as quickly. I see a bear that becomes a bull, a spider becoming a horseshoe crab, a snake head peeking out from behind a boulder. There is a rabbit darting away. Once passed, it has the tail of a fox. There is a horse which reinvents itself as a seahorse.

I think about how in the Psalms the poet sees clouds as taking on the distinctive shape of God's chariot (for instance, Psalm 104:3). I try to imagine what kind of chariot a seahorse might lead. I see a human-shaped figure with their hands above their head, resting or sleeping horizontally in the sky in the same pose that my infant daughter loves to sleep in these days. The hands become elongated and the body shrinks and suddenly the sleeping human is a crayfish swimming backwards against the sky's current. An elephant curls its trunk upwards into an upside-down question mark and opens its gummy mouth in a smile. Cloud continents reach out and connect for a bit, creating their own Bering Straits, while the invisible cloud tectonics break other cloud continents up and push them apart. I watch a bird cloud frozen in flight, a kestrel maybe, and see it begin to fade and then suddenly disappear completely, erased from the sky without leaving a trace as it passes into nothingness between me and the sun.

"Nature is a mutable cloud," as Emerson once put it, "which is always and never the same." When we attend to a cloud moving and changing in the sky, we are not just witnessing one little aspect of the world, but there's a sense in which we are witnessing the whole drama of the universe itself play out in a cloud. Like a cloud forming seemingly from out of nowhere when enough moisture has gathered together, so too the universe seemingly formed out of nowhere when enough energy had gathered together. Like how a cloud builds and builds in moisture until it explodes with rain and lightning, the matter and energy of the universe expands and expands, giving eruptive birth to new planets, stars, galaxies. Like how a cloud eventually loses all its moisture and disappears back into the nothingness of empty sky, so too the matter in this universe breaks down and dissolves back into the dark nothingness from whence it came. Everything that we see, including our own selves and bodies, is matter that has come together and configured itself in a unique way for a finite time—these maple trees that billow out of the Vermont earth where I stand, that butterfly that flits about, this grass that flourishes for a brief but glorious northern summer, these human bodies of ours, here on the receiving end of this gift of life for the time being, a small part of it all just like each water particle is a small part of the cloud.

If to witness a cloud is to witness the universe itself, it is also to witness ourselves as the universe witnessing itself, the human as the cosmos configuring itself into a posture of self-reflection. In Buddhist thought, the image of the cloud figures as a guiding metaphor for the nature of consciousness, as thoughts are said to be like clouds against the empty sky of mind (or no-mind, as the case may be). When we sit in Buddhist meditation, we sit to witness the natural processes of the human mind, which is to say that we sit to witness consciousness, or we sit to become conscious of consciousness, and aware of awareness, as we notice thoughts as they appear, as we sit with them while they sit with us, and as we notice them dart away back again into the void from whence they came. Like clouds, thoughts arise, unfold, change shape and mood, carry various messages, move, and then depart again from the sky of the mind. It is the whole drama or scene of both performance and audience that we call consciousness.

❋ ❋ ❋

The image of the "cloud of witnesses" in the Letter to the Hebrews derives historically from the world of athletics. The author is describing a scene reminiscent of how, in the ancient world, marathon races like the Olympics would reach their end in the stadium, with a final lap being made in the presence of the onlookers, cheering the exhausted runners on. This crowd is the image Hebrews calls a "great cloud of witnesses," and the race is the life of faith.

CLOUDS

In the preceding chapter, we read about how "by faith," Abel is in that cloud, "by faith," Noah is there, "by faith," Abraham and Sarah are there, "by faith," Rahab is there, "by faith," Moses and his mother Jochebed, and on and on. "By faith"—we're led to imagine for ourselves as we recall our own pantheon of those whose faith-formed lives have shaped our own. "By faith"—maybe your mother is there who taught you to say "this is the day that the Lord has made." "By faith"—maybe your grandfather is there who taught you about what it's like to walk through the valley of the shadow of death, fearing no evil. "By faith"—maybe your mentors or elders are there who taught you about the Jesus way of loving God and loving one's neighbor as oneself. "By faith"—maybe your spiritual heroes are there who showed you how to do justice, and love kindness, and walk humbly with your God.

"Therefore, since we are surrounded by so great a cloud of witnesses..."

It is curious that the metaphor used here to imagine the ancestors is clouds. More often than not in mythologies and cosmologies around the world, it's been the stars that have symbolized the ancestors. In ancient Greek philosophy, for example, Heraclitus gave voice to the common idea at the time of our astral immortality, that "when we die, we become stars in the sky." "Perhaps they are not stars in the sky," as an Inuit proverb puts it, "but rather openings where our loved ones shine down to let us know they are happy."

In the Bible, on the other hand, stars tend to be imagined less as representing those who came before us as representing the numerous ones that will come after us, as with the covenant God makes with Abraham, "to make your descendants as numerous as the stars in the sky" (Genesis 26:4). When the Bible does imagine the ancestors, they are closer to us than the stars in the sky, a little more down to earth, a little more present and impactful on our day-to-day living—less like distant stars and more like clouds hovering just overhead.

In this way, the Biblical understanding is akin to the Pueblo in the desert regions of the North American Southwest who turn to a class of supernatural beings that they call the Cloud People. The Cloud People are the spirits of the ancestors who lived good lives on earth, and so were blessed by the gods to be embodied as clouds in the afterlife. It is said that they form into clouds with the moisture from the last breath that they take, like the visible mini-clouds we breathe out in winter as the warm moisture within us cools and condenses and lingers for a moment in the cold, dry air. Theirs is a harsh desert landscape not unlike that in the Bible in which clouds can be the difference between famine and death and harvest and life. The Pueblo believe that if they pay proper respect to the dead, then their ancestors in the clouds, the Cloud People, will be kind and bring shade and moisture, rain and life.

＊ ＊ ＊

A type of Christian meditation known as the daily examen invites you, at the end of a given day, to reflect backwards in time on the events of the day in order to discern God's hand at work in the warp and weft of your life. Thinking about the cloud of witnesses, thinking back on all those who have shaped us, invites such a meditation practice, such an examen. We can begin where we are now, wondering—where have we come from? What's led to this moment? What have been the right steps, the accidents, the mistakes, the ancestors, the experiences? Everything that's happened up until now has set the stage for now. Therefore, we should "act our age," as the philosopher Joanna Macy likes to put it, reminding us that we're all made up of the stuff of this universe which is about 13.7 billion years old. We're made up of that wise, dark, bright, creative 13.7-billion-year-old stuff. We're made of it and we're surrounded by it. We're supported by it. We breathe it in. We look up at it in the clouds. We look out from it in our eyes. In a sense, throughout life we're cheered on by it, as if we were in the last lap of a race, hearing the cloud of witnesses urging us to a strong finish.

We need that cloud and that cloud needs us. It's almost impossible to imagine the end of an important athletic event like an Olympic race without cheering fans to witness it. I think about Usain Bolt breaking the 100m world record and striking that iconic lightning strike pose of victory as the crowd cheered with joy to have witnessed greatness. Without the crowd to witness it, such a moment would be incomplete. Usain Bolt needs the cheering crowd, as much as the cheering crowd needs Usain Bolt.

And so it is, our scripture suggests, for each of us as we run the races of our own lives. We need the cloud of witnesses to cheer us on as much as the cloud of witnesses needs us to run our race. We're both here to witness to one another. Which is to say that everything in God's creation needs everything else. We need the clouds, and we witness to the clouds, as much as the clouds need us and witness to us.

* * *

The intelligence of cloud cannot be overstated.

—Mark Strand, *89 Clouds*

I linger out this day with its parade of stratocumulus, its theater of God's glory on display, its spectacle of mindfulness. After seeing the crayfish and the rabbit with a fox's tail and God's seahorse chariot, I'm done looking for or caring about finding shapes and I rest in simple delight in the ever-shifting, ever-mutable, driftless, drifting cloudscape. The deep fjords of vivid blue sky covered by abstract shapes of white and gray-brown reminds me of something familiar and meaningful that I can't put my finger on at first. It's only weeks later, while reading about the fiftieth anniversary of the famous "Earthrise" photograph, that it strikes me—looking at the sky from below on a day like this is awfully similar to looking at a picture of planet Earth from outer space.

On Christmas Eve of 1968, the crew on the Apollo 8 mission made their fourth orbit around the moon, and as they made the turn towards home, the view of our little blue-white marble planet suddenly appearing against the ink black void was breathtaking and made for an instantly iconic photograph by crew member Bill Anders. With the barren gray moonscape in the foreground, and with a black nothing void spreading deep everywhere else, our home planet appears like a sparkling, surreal, gemstone gift. The image is widely and rightly hailed as a touchstone of the environmental movement and of humanity's budding awareness of our planetary unity and global interdependence.

Although ours is often described as a blue planet, the cloudy planet or the white planet would perhaps be a more apt natural description, because in that photo, and in just about any photo of the earth ever taken from space, clouds cover almost three-quarters of the scene. Deep blue water like the deep blue fjords of the sky today makes up for much of the rest of the picture. Faint, jagged outlines of the gray and brown of the continents play a distant third fiddle, much like the dusty gray-brown that speckles the white clouds today. While the blue seas give our planet its solid background canvas, and the gray-brown dirt gives it a suggestion of structure, it is the white abstract masterpiece of the ever-changing cloud cover that makes our planet such a seemingly stand-alone masterpiece of God's creativity as we sense it to be. In the images of earth from space, clouds are the singular artistic flourish and innovation.

In "Earthrise," the clouds show us a planet alive and on the move, a planet where things are happening, an energy orb of spontaneity and possibility that also happens to be beautiful and in a fragile balance. They also, I think, show us a planet that is aware, and awake. We need each other and we need to witness each other. It is all one big cloud of witnesses, which is one big cloud of consciousness, and we're cheered on by it, and we cheer it on, and we look up at it, and we look down upon it, and thoughts and clouds rise and fall, and consciousness yawns and stretches itself out, as our planet slowly and desperately wakes up.

4

JESUS RAYS

I have relinquished all that ties me to the world,
but the one thing that still haunts me is the beauty of the sky.

—Yoshida Kenk,
A Cup of Sake Beneath the Cherry Trees

When I greet the clouds on this gentle Vermont summer morning, I find a classic cumulus sky, the cauliflower heads arranged with enough space around them to each be the subject of their own still life, and together as an ensemble they add a dimension of telegraphic distance to the sky, creating a sense of horizon and its emotional pull more powerful than even the best masters of Renaissance painting with their linear perspective could manage. Cloud shadows are promenading over the fields, the grass is sashaying in the wind, the clover and Queen Anne's lace look like confetti in the sunlight in one moment and then just a moment later look like stars and constellations as a cloud shadow darkens over them.

CLOUDS

A few larger clouds seem to have pitched their tents over the Adirondack Mountains in the distance to the west, content with their lot in life. A faint band of cirrus high overhead at first also seems fixed in the sky as if etched in permanent ink, but upon closer gaze the wisps at its edges are unfurling, just like their Latin name, which means "curl," as in the way that ringlets or curling locks of hair flow in the wind. Just above the cirrus, there's a cloud that's changing even faster as an airplane heads north and east towards Montreal, leaving behind a rapidly evolving and eventually disappearing contrail line in the sky, a decidedly geometric and modernist cloud compared to the rounded cumulus and the coy cirrus. Feeling like my words are falling short of the beauty of the moment, I take solace in what Arizona writer Terri Guillemets once said about clouds. "Why do I love clouds?" she mused. "Because you can't save a cloud like you can save a leaf or a flower or a rock—clouds are now."

The connection between clouds and time is emblematic of the more general relationship humans tend to sense between the sky and time. For many cultures and for much of history, the sky is where humans have looked to tell the time. From the regular movement of the stars and the moon we get astronomy, calendars, chronological time, Stonehenge, and sun dials. From the erratic appearance and metamorphosis of the clouds we get meteorology, derived from the Greek *meteora*, meaning a type of kairotic moment when something suddenly appears in the sky, like a meteor. In Latin, *tempus* means both weather and time. In English we have temporal and tempest. In French *le temps*, and in Spanish *el tiempo*, both meaning time and weather.

While clouds tend to tell time more often as *kairos* than as *chronos*, in the Bible clouds do have a historical sense as well, as reminders of the past, of that which has come before us—for instance, Noah's rainbow or the "cloud of witnesses"—and when we turn to the end of the Bible in the New Testament, both to the end of the account of the life of Jesus as well as to the apocalyptic end in Revelation, clouds appear in a futural sense—as signs pointing ahead to what is yet to come.

Every now and then in the Bible we find attempts to ponder the very end—the end of this world as we know and can comprehend it. These moments in the Bible are known as apocalyptic literature. Apocalypse is a word with Greek roots that means uncovering or revealing, like when the clouds finally depart and you see the mountaintop.

The first apocalyptic vision in the Bible is in the Old Testament book of Daniel, a highly imaginative text in which the prophet uses dreams and dream interpretation, along with other spiritual practices like fasting, to peer into and prophesy the future. In Daniel's vision, God will appear at the end of time and send someone like a savior to earth to set up a final order of justice and righteousness. And the way the savior will come, as Daniel sees it, will be as "one like a human being coming on the clouds of heaven" (Daniel 7:13).

While it can often be difficult to know what to do with, or what to make of apocalyptic visions like this, the context here is that the Jewish community Daniel writes within was being held in a vise grip of oppression by the Roman Empire about 200 years before Jesus. The world for them, as it has for so many others throughout history, must have felt like an unjust and chaotic place. It must have felt far from their deepest hopes and dreams for what better, more beautiful world could be possible. And so, the prophet speaks to the people about the distant future. The prophet peers towards that more beautiful world. And his vision is that even if the world as it is now seems unjust and confusing, God's justice and God's truth will get the last word. The apocalyptic vision then is a hopeful vision, because the end belongs to God, not to the powers-that-be of today. To the question "What's going to happen? What's the end going to be like?" the prophet proclaims, "God is going to happen. The end will be with God. The end will be God."

While Daniel's vision is a unique, standalone apocalyptic moment in the Hebrew Bible, in the New Testament his vision played a critical role in shaping the early Christian community's understanding of what the end times would be like. For the early Jesus followers and writers of the Gospels, the vague "human one" that Daniel mentions is identified as Jesus, and that phrase "human one" becomes the main title that the New Testament uses to name Jesus—the "Son of Man." There are references to Daniel 7 in the other Gospels as well, but in Mark, during Jesus's trial, he's asked if he is the Messiah, the Savior. "I am," Jesus responds, "and you will see the Son of Man seated at the right hand of Power and coming with the clouds of heaven" (Mark 14:62).

The New Testament builds on Daniel's cloud apocalypse in the description of Jesus's Ascension in Acts 1. For forty days, the resurrected Christ is described as giving his final teachings and instructions. The only content of the dialogue given suggests that time and timing was a major theme of the discussion, as at one point the disciples ask Jesus if this is the time that Israel will be restored. They are asking about the apocalypse, about what things will be like at the end of time and about when that time will come. As he does elsewhere when asked questions about the apocalypse, Jesus says here, "that's not for you to know" (Acts 1:7). That's not for you to know because the ultimate end is in God's hands. The ultimate end is with God. The ultimate end is God.

And then suddenly he's gone. Right after these last words, "as they were watching, he was lifted up, and a cloud took him out of their sight" (Acts 1:9). The King James Version describes it with a bit more poetry: "while they beheld, he was taken up; and a cloud received him." The disciples stare up at the now suddenly vacant sky into a world that feels drained of meaning. Two angels, or strangers at least, tap them on the shoulder. "Why do you stand here looking into the sky?" they ask. "This same Jesus, who has been taken from you into heaven, will come back in the same way you have seen him go into heaven" (Acts 1:11). In other words, the Son of Humanity, the human one, the one who left into the clouds will come back with the clouds.

✳ ✳ ✳

There's a breathtakingly beautiful cloud phenomenon that every now and then occurs in the late afternoon, when the skies are nearly filled with a stratocumulus cloud field, with just a handful of small stripes in the sky here and there. The sun itself can't be seen behind the clouds. But visible rays from the sun stream through the gaps in the clouds and beam and fan out down from the sun to the cloud-shadowed earth. From our perspective down here as we look up, the rays converge in the obscured sun, which, because of their perspectival effect, seems like it should be much closer to us than it is. The rays make the sun appear to be just behind the clouds, not the 100 million miles away that it actually is. Crepuscular rays, named after the twilight time of day when they appear, are what these are technically called, although they go by many other wonderful names as well. Ropes of Maui are what the Maori in New Zealand call them, named after the trickster god who is said to use these rays like ropes to try to stop the sun from setting and so prolong the light of the day. The Greeks had a phrase for these beams—"sun drawing water"—because they thought that was how water was pulled up into the sky like from a straw to form rain, an early attempt to describe the evaporation process. Jews call them Jacob's Ladder. Buddha rays are what Buddhists call them. And for Christians, these are known as Jesus rays.

"Look," John of Patmos writes in the opening chapter of the last book of the Bible, "he is coming with the clouds, and every eye will see him" (Revelation 1:7). And on that ultimate day, God will be here with us in a down-to-earth, ecological, personal way—God will wipe away every tear from our eyes, and death will be no more, and mourning and weeping and suffering will be no more, and there will be a new heaven and a new earth. And the sky will be a cloud savior sky, as Jesus rays stream from the beautiful sun through the beautiful clouds and kiss this beautiful earth.

EPILOGUE
Loving God through Loving the World

DRIFTLESS AREA, WISCONSIN

There is only one world, a world that God loves.
Since God loves it, we not only can but should.
In fact, loving the world (not God alone), or rather,
loving God through loving the world, is the Christian way.

—SALLIE MCFAGUE

I t is the full Buck Moon, and the apex of summer in Wisconsin. Born on the full Winter Moon at the end of November, our daughter Reverie turned eight moons old today. We've been calling each full moon her "Faye birthday," in honor of her middle name and its etymological connection to the faeries and nature spirits. To celebrate, our family of three went for a hike in the community forest we've come to know and love just a couple of hills over from where we've been living this past pandemic year in the Driftless area of southwest Wisconsin. Stretching from a bit west of Madison to a bit south of Minneapolis, and including some of the northeastern corner of Iowa and the northwestern corner of Illinois, the topography of the Driftless area is unlike the rest of the Midwest. Here, rather than cornfields and a landscape flattened by glaciation and spotted with lakes, you'll find a rugged, ancient, and enigmatic terrain of hills upon hills and steep limestone valleys carved by cold spring fed streams. Here you'll find the highest concentration of trout streams anywhere in the world, the highest concentration of Native American effigy mounds anywhere in the country, and the squeakiest cheese curds around.

"Drift" is the technical term for what glaciers leave behind when they recede—erratics, boulders, eskers, drumlins, sand, gravel. This area is called driftless because it lacks all such evidence of glaciation, especially from the last ice age that scrapped flat the rest of the Upper Midwest twelve thousand years ago. The pocket of the Driftless area in southwest Wisconsin is thought to be even more ancient still, as geological evidence suggests that this region has been untouched by glaciers stretching back at least 2.5 million years. While in human terms driftless suggests a person who is aimless and wandering, in terms of this area it names a landscape that has not wavered or changed much over time, at least compared to its surrounding regions. As such, the Driftless feels like it holds forgotten secrets, like it holds complexities and multitudes, and like it moves at a different pace than the rest of the region, much like how people here drive slow on the backroads, where the next passenger is just as likely to be an Amish buggy, a wild turkey, a family of deer, or an ATV. It is a wonderful place to get lost for a while, to dream driftless dreams, to ponder geologic time, and to meditate with the earth element.

As this is high summer, the native prairie ecosystem that fills the fields of our community forest is in full swing. We begin our hike in the prairie under the high sun as we walk through fields of wild bergamot, oxeye daisy, Indian cup, yarrow, yellow coneflower, and prairie fleabane, among other flowering perennials. While the bees and butterflies are smitten with the pollen, we're sidetracked by perfectly ripe thickets of black raspberry and blackberry. Before the prairie portion of the trail ends, a side trail takes you deep into the coulee forest, where the temperature drops and you can find alpine plants enjoying the natural air conditioning effect of the cool, algific talus slopes that suggest the presence of sinkholes, caves, and groundwater springs underfoot. We hike past the spot where we gathered morels and ramps earlier in the spring, now covered in nettle and mayapple with the occasional blue bellflower rising above the floor canopy. We clear the ridge and make our way back down to the prairie below.

The moment of transition from the dark forest back to the open prairie is always a moment of astonishment for me. Before making the turn, I pause in the last pocket of cool forest shade. With Reverie asleep on my chest in her baby carrier, I too rest my eyes and let everything go dark for a moment—trying to bracket and set aside thought and mental striving, assumptions about life and the world, religion, language, everything. A moment of emptying, like entering a cloud of unknowing, like groping around in the darkness of nonbeing, like befriending the void.

As I open my eyes, I make the turn from forest back to prairie. The trees cast a half curtain of shadow across the trail just in front of me, but beyond that the world opens with light, and it is as suddenly and surprisingly bright as when the opening moments of a film are first projected on the dark, blank screen. With my eyes closed, there was nothing, and now with them open, everything in its summer glory overwhelms the eyes and the senses. It is too much. And delightfully so. It is dizzying and blinding. It is magnificent.

And there's more. The world is not for one moment static, but moves and is alive with constant change. A red cardinal zips across the field. The grass sways with the wind and hums with insect life. Summer cumulus float over the field like a herd of turtles on the slow go. The trees catch the light breeze and the forest as a whole swells like a green sea. Things appear, change, and then disappear. If I stood here long enough, I could see the wave of the prairie lap against the hillside forest, going up the hill for a time, back down for a time, and then back up. I could watch the hills themselves come and go. I could watch again and again the fullness of summer fade away in fall into the emptiness of winter, only for presence to emerge again in spring. With my eyes closed, and then open as I gaze out mirrorlike, as an opening of consciousness through which the world reflects and registers itself, I sense the essential connection between the nothingness from which things emerge and the field of presence in the fullness of its glory. I sense the absence from which presence steps forth for a brief time, before dipping back into the empty pool of the void, and I know that I too am part of that absence-presence continuum, that churning and turning of life, that tilling of the soil of nothingness from which the flowering field of the world is born.

✳ ✳ ✳

Alongside the nearly universal four classical elements of nature, sometimes a fifth element is proposed. The ancient Greeks called it æther, ether, or the quintessence (in Latin). They imagined it as a substance like pure air, or translucent air, like the air that filled the universe beyond the earth's atmosphere, like the air that the gods breathed. In the Japanese *godai* account of things, there are also five elements, and the fifth element is the void (*ku*). The void is the absence, the hole at the center of things, the nothingness from which the ten thousand things emerge and to which they return. The void is the empty space that atomic physics suggests makes up ninety-nine percent of every atom. The void is the ninety-eight percent of the universe that astronomy suggests is made up of non-observable dark matter and dark energy. The void is what you're looking for when you don't know what you're looking for, only that you're looking for something. The void is what we try to avoid when we distract ourselves with our business rather than sit with the wordless mystery that is always with us and within us. There are a million daily ways to try to fill or forget the void, and yet there is no way to fill or forget it. "There is a God-shaped void," as Blaise Pascal put it, "within the heart of every human being." And so, here we are as we glide through this universe, us and this void.

The void is nothing, and yet it is a gracious, generative sort of nothing. We open our eyes, and the empty mirror of the mind finds not dark nothingness, but the world in all of its flickering beauty, the bright burn of being, the searing truth of something rather than nothing. And so we know that while the void is absence, it is an absence that makes presence possible. In searching for the God-shaped void, in searching for the invisibility of God, we find the universe as it is, we find the visibility of the world. We, who are children of the void, are at the same time heirs to a glimmering world. When we open our eyes in this way, we can find ourselves nearly blinded by a ravenous and rapturous gratitude for the earth and its abundance. We open our eyes and we can find ourselves falling in love with the world with the type of irresistible love that we describe as love at first sight. It's not a love we can choose to have or not have, but a love that has us, that holds us, that keeps us here and awake and present to our creative task of helping the world describe, understand, and celebrate itself as it comes into being and translates itself from absence to presence, seeking its fullness of expression. By embracing the void, by befriending it, we come back to the world with a more properly ecstatic appreciation for what is, and a more urgent call to attend to its flourishing.

✳ ✳ ✳

Earth's the right place for love:
I don't know where it's likely to go better.

—Robert Frost

With Reverie asleep for the night after celebrating her eighth moon, we step out to gaze at the Buck Moon as it rises in the southeast over the dark Driftless hills. The moon is a pumpkin orange tonight, and not because it is a supermoon or a blood moon, but because wildfires have been raging out west, their smoke casting an ominous glow around the sun by day and the moon by night. We are on pace to set yet another mark for the hottest summer, and hottest year, on record. Other species, our fellow creatures and evolutionary journey mates on this planet, are disappearing, becoming extinct at an unfathomable rate, each one taking away a bit of God's glory with them as they go. Meanwhile, the richest people on the planet are busy making plans to leave earth and colonize Mars, among other extraterrestrial dreams.

With all due respect to the daring creativity and adventurous spirit that seeks to push the frontier of human presence further out into the solar system and beyond, the real frontier at the moment for our species lies in our quest to dwell with this earth in a mutually beneficial, mutually beautiful way. The real frontier, the real edge of discovery, can be found within the longings of each human heart, as we will only ever learn to treat beautifully and carefully and compassionately what we first love truly and deeply. The climate crisis reveals a misplaced longing. We seem to be in love with something other than the earth and its flourishing. If we discover or rediscover a boundless love for the earth, it will be for our species, as it has been said, like discovering fire for the second time.

From the climate crisis to the sixth mass extinction event that marks the beginning of the Anthropocene, what is this critical moment in the history of our journey as a species but an opportunity and an urgency to fall more deeply in love with the earth? The rivers, the mountains, the trees, the clouds, all of it. This, then, I believe, is the call of our times that is coming to us from the direction of the earth—to love God with all our heart and with all our soul and with all our strength and with all our mind. To love God through loving the world.

NOTES

EPIGRAPHS

p.   v, ¶ 1   Unless otherwise noted, scripture references are from the New Revised Standard Version (NRSV). In this case the translation of Job 12:8a is my own. It is inspired by other translations of *siach* (שׂיח) as *commune, meditate, pray, muse.*

p.   v, ¶ 2   Wendell Berry, *Sex, Economy, Freedom & Community* (New York: Pantheon, 1993), 103.

p.   v, ¶ 3   Sallie McFague, *Life Abundant: Rethinking Theology and Economy for a Planet in Peril* (Minneapolis: Fortress Press, 2000), 13.

p.   v, ¶ 4   Simone Weil, *Waiting on God*, trans. Emma Craufurd (Routledge: 1951), 60.

p.   v, ¶ 5   Henry David Thoreau, *The Journal, 1837–1861* (New York: New York Review Books Classics, 2009), 117.

PROLOGUE: GOD'S TWO BOOKS

p.   2, ¶ 1   Wallace Stevens, "Of the Surface of Things," in *The Collected Poems of Wallace Stevens* (New York: Vintage Books, 2015), 60.

p.   4, ¶ 1   As quoted in *The Green Bible* (New York: HarperCollins Publishers, 2008), 1-101.

p. 5, ¶ 3   As quoted in Belden Lane, *Backpacking with the Saints: Wilderness Hiking as Spiritual Practice* (Oxford: Oxford University Press, 2014), 229.

p. 6, ¶ 1   As quoted in *The Green Bible*.

p. 6, ¶ 2   Thomas Aquinas, *Summa Contra Gentiles*, II.3.1, II.3.6.

p. 6, ¶ 3   I am indebted to Lyndal Roper for her insight into Luther's "Real Presence" theory. See: Lyndal Roper, *Martin Luther: Renegade and Prophet* (New York: Random House, 2017).

p. 7, ¶ 2   Martin Luther, "That These Words of Christ, 'This is My Body,' etc. Still Stand Firm Against the Fanatics," in *Luther's Works* (St. Louis: Concordia, 1959), 37:57.

p. 9, ¶ 2   Henry David Thoreau, *The Natural History Essays* (Utah: Gibs Smith, 1980), 93.

CREATION ELEMENT INTERLUDE: WATER

p. 14, ¶ 2   Mircea Eliade, *Patterns in Comparative Religion* (University of Nebraska Press, 1996), 188.

p. 15, ¶ 4   *Tao Te Ching*, trans. Derek Lin (Woodstock, VT: SkyLight, 2006), verse 78.

p. 16, ¶ 3   Henry David Thoreau, *A Week on the Concord and Merrimack Rivers* (Penguin Classics, 1998), 269.

THE SOURCE: RIVERS OF PARADISE

p. 17, epigraph "The Mountain Poems of Hsieh Ling-yün," from the website of translator David Hinton, accessed April 27, 2022. https:// www.davidhinton.net/hsieh-ling-yun-sample-poems.

MOTHER RIVER

p. 27, epigraph Amit Kalantri, *Wealth of Words*, https://www.goodreads.com/quotes/9179773-if-the-earth-is-a-mother-then-rivers-are-her.

LIVING WATERS (DOWN IN THE RIVER TO PRAY)

p. 36, ¶ 1   Martin Luther's *Sindflutgebet*, or "flood prayer," can be found in many Lutheran books of worship. It is quoted here from: Ronald Byers, *The Sacraments in Biblical*

NOTES

Perspective (Atlanta: Presbyterian Publishing Corporation, 2011), 23.

p. 36, ¶ 1   From Martin Luther's *Large Catechism.*

p. 39, ¶ 1   "River out of Eden: Water, Ecology, and the Jordan River in Jewish Tradition," Ecopeace/Friends of the Earth Middle East (FOEME), Second Edition, 2014. https://old.eco peaceme.org/wp-content/uploads/2020/10/14036834380 %5E%5ESource book_Judiasm_FINAL.pdf

p. 39, ¶ 2   *Tao Te Ching,* Verse 8, trans. Stephen Mitchell (New York: HarperCollins, 1994).

APOCALYPTIC HOPE:
WATERSHED DISCIPLESHIP & THE ROUND RIVER

p. 41, epigraph   Mary Oliver, *Upstream: Selected Essays* (Penguin Books, 2019), 154.

p. 42, ¶ 1   Orphic Hymn to Pan, in Thomas Taylor, *The Mystical Hymns of Orpheus* (C. Whittingham, 1824), 36.

p. 43, ¶ 3   Norman Maclean, *A River Runs Through It* (Chicago: University of Chicago Press, 1976), 161.

p. 44, ¶ 1   Aldo Leopold, *Round River* (Oxford: Oxford University Press, 1993), 158.

p. 47, ¶ 2   Ched Myers, *Watershed Discipleship: Reinhabiting Bioregional Faith and Practice* (Eugene: Cascade Books, 2016).

p. 49, ¶ 1   Hafiz, *The Gift,* trans. Daniel Ladinsky (New York: Penguin Compass, 1999), 3.

CREATION ELEMENT INTERLUDE: FIRE

p. 52, ¶ 1   Heraclitus, Fragment 30, in *The Columbia Dictionary of Quotations* (New York: Columbia University Press, 1989), 335.

p. 53, ¶ 3   Mircea Eliade, *Patterns in Comparative Religion* (Lincoln: University of Nebraska Press, 1996), 99.

THE THREE RULES OF MOUNTAINEERING

p. 55, epigraph   Gregory of Nyssa, *The Life of Moses,* trans. Abraham J. Malherbe and Everett Furguson (New York: Paulist Press, 1978), 93.

p. 56, ¶ 4   Robert Macfarlane, *Mountains of the Mind: Adventures in Reaching the Summit* (New York: Vintage, 2004), 193.

p. 60, ¶ 2   Soren Kierkegaard, *Fear and Trembling and The Book on Adler* (New York: Everyman's Library, 1994), 28.

p. 61, ¶ 5   As quoted in: Wade Davis, *Into the Silence: The Great War, Mallory, and the Conquest of Everest* (New York: Vintage, 2012), 406.

p. 64, ¶ 4   Henry David Thoreau, *A Week on the Concord and Merrimack Rivers; Walden; The Maine Woods; Cape Cod* (New York: Library Classics of the United States, 1985), 646.

THE LIVING MOUNTAIN OF GOD

p. 67, epigraph *Mishkan T'filah: A Reform Siddur* (New York: Central Conference of Reformed Rabbis, 2007), 81.

p. 68, ¶ 1   Belden Lane, *The Solace of Fierce Landscapes: Exploring Desert and Mountain Spirituality* (Oxford: Oxford University Press, 2007), 43.

p. 70, ¶ 1   These and the following are from: Nan Shepherd, *The Living Mountain* (Canongate Canons, 2011).

p. 76, ¶ 5   For the time being, you can find this photo here: https:// charlotte peacock.co.uk/nan-shepherd/nan-shepherd-works-by-charlotte-peacock/nan-shepherd-poet-peaks-charlotte-peacock/.

THINKING LIKE A MOUNTAIN
(A CLIMBING HISTORY OF CHRIST)

p. 79, epigraph Thomas Merton, *Conjectures of a Guilty Bystander* (New York: Doubleday, 1966), 140–42.

p. 83, ¶ 1   Irenaeus of Lyon (c. 130–c. 202), *Against Heresies*, book 4, 20.7.

p. 84, ¶ 4   Aldo Leopold, *A Sand County Almanac* (New York: Ballantine Books, 1970), 137.

PANORAMA OF THE PROMISED LAND

p. 87, epigraph John Muir, *Nature Writings* (Library of America, 1997), 202.

p. 88, ¶ 3   Albert W. Palmer, *The Mountain Trail and Its Message* (Boston: The Pilgrim Press, 1911)

NOTES

CREATION ELEMENT INTERLUDE: EARTH

p. 95, epigraph   Hannah Arendt, *The Human Condition* (Chicago: The University of Chicago Press, 1958), 2.

p. 97, ¶ 1   Angelus Silesius, *The Cherubinic Wanderer* (New York: Paulist Press, 1986), 54.

p. 98, ¶ 1   Thomas Merton, *New Seeds of Contemplation* (New York: New Directions, 2007), 29.

TREES AND BEAUTY: ECOLOGICAL ETHICS AS AESTHETICS

p. 99, epigraph   Rachel Carson, *Lost Woods* (Boston: Beacon Press, 2010), 94.

p. 110, ¶ 3   Richard Higgins, *Thoreau and the Language of Trees* (Berkeley: University of California Press, 2017), 115, 111.

p. 111, ¶ 2   *The Essential Rumi*, trans. Coleman Barks (New York: HarperCollins, 1995), 36.

ABRAHAM AND SARAH ON HOSPITALITY: PRACTICING OAK ETHICS

p. 113, epigraph   Rameshwar Dass, *Be Love Now* (New York: Harper-Collins, 2010), 23.

p. 114, ¶ 2   Peter Wohlleben, *The Hidden Life of Trees* (New York: Penguin Books Limited, 2016).

p. 121, ¶ 3   Henry David Thoreau, *October, Or Autumnal Tints* (New York: W. W. Norton, 2012), 89.

TREE MEDICINE: ELIJAH UNDER THE BROOM TREE

p. 123, epigraph   As quoted in: Heidi Neumark, *Breathing Space: A Spiritual Journey in the South Bronx* (Boston: Beacon Press, 2012), 97.

p. 126, ¶ 2   Eve Ensler, *In the Body of the World* (New York: Picador, 2014), 101.

p. 129, ¶ 4   R. H. Blyth, trans. and ed., *Haiku (Volume II): Spring* (New York: Angelico Press, 2021).

EVERY TREE A TREE OF LIFE

p. 131, epigraph   While it is difficult to track down this popular quote, a discussion of it can be found here: *The Cambridge Companion to Martin Luther* (Cambridge: Cambridge University Press, 2003), 162.

NOTES

p. 132, ¶ 3	Leopold, *A Sand County Almanac*, 73.
p. 136, ¶ 2	Damian Carrington, "Global Warming of Oceans Equivalent to an Atomic Bomb per Second," *The Guardian*, January 7, 2019, https://www.theguardian.com /environment/2019/jan /07/global-warming-of-oceans-equivalent-to-an-atomic-bomb-per-second.
p. 138, ¶ 1	Frank Prevot, illustrated by Aurelia Fronty, *Wangari Maathai: The Woman Who Planted Millions of Trees* (Watertown, MA: Charlesbridge Publishing, 2015).

CREATION ELEMENT INTERLUDE: AIR

p. 139, epigraph	Epigraph from *The Green Bible* (New York: HarperCollins, 2008).
p. 140, ¶ 2	As quoted in Esther De Wall, *The Celtic Way of Prayer* (Syracuse, NY: Image, 1999), xv.
p. 141, ¶ 2	John O'Donohue, *Four Elements: Reflections on Nature* (New York: Harmony, 2011).

THE HEAVENS ARE TELLING THE GLORY OF GOD

p. 143, epigraph	Ovid, *Metamorphoses*, book I:68–88 "Humankind," as quoted in Peter Matthiessen, *The Snow Leopard* (New York: Penguin Classics, 2008), 7.
p. 144, ¶ 1	Ralph Waldo Emerson, *Journal*, 25 May 1843, as quoted in Gavin Pretor-Pinney, *The Cloudspotter's Guide* (New York: Penguin, 2007), 304.
p. 144, ¶ 2	C. S. Lewis, *Reflections on the Psalms* (London: Collins, 1958), 56.
p. 145, ¶ 4	Jan Brogan, "Looking at the Sky May Change Your Entire POV," *Boston Globe*, January 7, 2013, https://www .bostonglobe.com/lifestyle/2013/01/07/looking-sky-may-change-your-entire-pov/vKZTzCC7EqL1QRD kw1N7rK/story.html.
p. 147, ¶ 4	From the website of artist James Turrell, https://james turrell.com/work/type/skyspace/.
p. 149, ¶ 2	Michael Govan interview with James Turrell, *Interview* Magazine, May 23, 2011, https://www.interview magazine.com/art/james-turell.

N O T E S

SIGNS OF THE TIMES

p. 153, epigraph As quoted in Gavin Pretor-Pinney, *The Cloudspotter's Guide* (New York: Penguin, 2007), 77.

p. 155, ¶ 1 *The New Century Hymnal: UCC Pew Edition* (Cleveland: Pilgrim Press, 1997).

p. 155, ¶ 2 "Joyful, Joyful, We Adore You" (public domain), *The New Century Hymnal: UCC Pew Edition* (Cleveland: Pilgrim Press, 1997).

p. 155, ¶ 3 "Sun of My Soul, O Savior Dear" (public domain), *The New Century Hymnal: UCC Pew Edition* (Cleveland: Pilgrim Press, 1997).

p. 155, ¶ 4 "When I Survey in Wonder," *The New Century Hymnal: UCC Pew Edition* (Cleveland: Pilgrim Press, 1997), translation ©The Pilgrim Press.

p. 155, ¶ 5 "Touch the Earth Lightly." Words: Shirley Erena Murray, ©1992 Hope Publishing Company, www.hope publishing.com. All rights reserved. Used by permission.

p. 155, ¶ 6 "We Worship You God (All Glorious Above)," *The New Century Hymnal: UCC Pew Edition* (Cleveland: Pilgrim Press, 1997), word alterations ©The Pilgrim Press.

p. 157, ¶ 1 Paul Tillich, *Systematic Theology*, vol. 2 (Chicago: University of Chicago Press, 1957), 9.

p. 158, ¶ 3 Fred Pearce, "Why Clouds Are the Key to New Troubling Projections on Warming," *Yale Environment 360*, February 5, 2020, https://e360.yale.edu/features/why-clouds-are-the-key-to-new-troubling-projections-on-warming/.

CLOUD OF WITNESSES

p. 162, ¶ 3 Ralph Waldo Emerson, *Nature and Selected Essays* (New York: Penguin Classics, 2003), 156.

p. 166, ¶ 3 Mark Strand, *89 Clouds* (New York: ACA Galleries, 1999), number 58.

JESUS RAYS

p. 169, epigraph Kenko, *A Cup of Sake Beneath the Cherry Trees* (New York: Penguin, 2015).

NOTES

p. 170, ¶ 1   Terri Guillemets, "Sunshine Journal," July 4, 2009,
https://www.terriguillemets.com/tag/clouds/.

EPILOGUE: LOVING GOD THROUGH LOVING THE WORLD

p. 175, epigraph   Sallie McFague, *Life Abundant: Rethinking Theology and
Economy for a Planet in Peril* (Minneapolis: Fortress Press,
2000), 13.

p. 179, ¶ 1   This commonly attributed quote is most likely a para-
phrase derived from Blaise Pascal, *Pensees* (New York:
Penguin Books, 1966), 75.

p. 179, ¶ 3   Robert Frost, "Birches," in *The Poetry of Robert Frost:
The Collected Poems* (Henry Holt and Company, 1979),
122.

p. 180, ¶ 2   Pierre Teilhard de Chardin, *Toward the Future*
(New York: HarperOne, 2002), 87.